Teachers Mad

Christopher North

chipmunkapublishing
the mental health publisher

All rights reserved, no part of this publication may be reproduced by any means, electronic, mechanical photocopying, documentary, film or in any other format without prior written permission of the publisher.

>Published by
>Chipmunkapublishing
>United Kingdom

http://www.chipmunkapublishing.com

Copyright © 2021 Christopher North

ISBN   978-1-78382-267-6

Teacher's Mad

Chapter 1: St Mary's

St Mary's hadn't seen a teacher like Joseph before: as Joseph got out of the car, he looked up at the sky pensively and spots of rain began to drip from the heavens. He wondered how it was all going to end. The skies darkened over the aging school that loomed up before him. The old oak tree stood intransigent, rooted to the ground. He walked up to the main school entrance not knowing what to expect. He wondered what was in store behind the doors.

It was nearing the end of the academic year at St Mary's and thoughts were turning towards recruitment for the up and coming Autumn Term. They had received an application for em-ployment from a young man who looked most promising on paper and so they had decided to invite him in for an interview. As Joseph was about to open the main entrance door it violently flew open in his face and Mrs Bylaw sprung forth and was gone. Joseph managed to catch the door before it slammed shut again and he entered discreetly.

Inside, he looked around for the reception area; there were signs but it took him a moment to see them. Recollecting his senses, he noticed a big red arrow directing him to his place of need. He passed a flight of stairs leading to higher places and went through another set of doors; he tentatively approached the reception desk and cautiously stated his name and pur-pose:
"Hi, my name is Joseph, I've come for an interview."

"Right, we are expecting you. Take a seat in the waiting area and someone will be out to see you in a moment," replied the receptionist.

Joseph sat down on a rather uncomfortable brown chair until his time arrived. He waited nervously; his hands sweated as he rubbed his fingers and palm together with agitation. He could slide his thumb and second finger against one another with no friction whatsoever. Finally he was summoned and led to a room with a circular table and three people positioned around it.

Mrs Standard, the Deputy Head, sat opposite the vacant chair, Mrs Grouch, the Head of De-partment, sat adjacent to the vacant chair and Mrs Faith, the School Chaplain, sat opposite Mrs Grouch, and then there was a man (he stood in the background). He did not reveal his status but tweaked his moustache. Each of the ladies lay in wait curious to put a face to the application received.

Mrs Standard led proceedings; she was a hearty woman of generous proportions. Her love for the sound of her own voice was only bettered by the actual act of enunciation. Mrs Grouch also liked to talk but her love of the spoken word also depended upon the ceremony of making a brew. Mrs Standard would love to deliver her lines in a loud deliberate free standing act of expression where props, whether it be a cup or saucer, were superfluous. Mrs Grouch, in contrast, would like to ingratiate and weave her words with sarcasm and the refreshing taste of a hot cup of tea.

Mrs Faith did not care for gossip (of course) but spoke the word of the Lord. She spoke with reverence which was really pride in herself and determination: she dipped and rose in her discourse as all good people of the cloth do when wishing to distinguish the divine from the commonplace.

The questions started with purpose, they were designed to illicit assurances that this person, Joseph, was suitable for the post of Teacher of English. Mrs Standard wanted assurances that he could fulfil the pastoral side of the job; could he take care of the needs of children in the proper fashion? Mrs Grouch was keen to see his certificates proving his subject expertise and Mrs faith wanted him to know that the Lord was on her side.

He answered each question to their satisfaction but then it came to that question; the one that is usually at the end and the one that often tells you the most about an unknown person:
"Now, is there anything that you would like to ask us?" Said Mrs Standard, who sat opposite Joseph staring him full in the face and dwarfing him in the process.
"Yes, I do apologise, but can I use your toilet?"
"Toilet, toilet, well yes," replied Mrs Standard in surprise and amusement. "I did not expect that question. If that was a child asking the answer would be no, stay in your seat till its break-time but since it's you, you'll find the facilities on the left as you step out of the door, then over on the right-hand side."
"I'm sorry, I forgot to go before," said Joseph apologetically. "I can see that the school is a good school but if I could just excuse myself it would be most appreciated."
"Don't worry. If you would like to take a seat in the waiting area once you've visited the little boys-room that will give us time to come to a decision as to whether we feel you are a suitable candidate for employment. Okay?"
"Yes, thank you," said Joseph keen to exit.

Joseph set off for the little boys-room whilst the ladies clucked around the table. Wild amuse-ment reigned as they came to terms with the unusual question put by the candidate. Even the man in the room jeopardised his silence to muse at such a request. His hand dropped from his mouth which had been stroking his moustache and it revealed an embarrassed smile.

The ladies clucked and ruminated over the merits of the young man. Had he the skills to cope with the job? Would he survive in an all-female department? Did they want a man in their de-partment? So many questions to cluck over. What joy! Finances were paramount of course. In a time when budgets were stretched to the limits and demands were put on school perfor-mance, the appointment of a newly qualified teacher would save them money; money saved here could be put there, money put there could improve the school elsewhere. So yes. Let's give him a try. Lets give him a chance.

Joseph meanwhile heaved. He had placed himself fairly onto the toilet seat. His trousers were down around his ankles and his pants lay on top where they had fallen. He squirmed, he squeezed, he bent forward and pushed with all his might. His face went a bright red, beads of sweat were forming on his brow, his eyes balls were threatening to divorce their sockets, but no, it would not come.

It could not come. It was too big. It was buried deep down in the unconscious where lurks a terrible silence. He relented. He gave a deep sigh and cleaned his bottom. He pulled up his pants, he pulled up his trousers, he unlocked the cubicle door that concealed trouble and trot-ted over to the sink. Joseph washed his hands and the sweat from his brow. He glanced up momentarily at his reflection to check that he was still

himself. He took a paper towel from the dispenser and dried his hands. He then opened the door and left the toilet with a sense of unease. What was in store for him? How was it all going to turn out? Again he took himself over to the rather uncomfortable brown seat and awaited his fate. He waited. His hands were sweating again. And then out popped the silent man: "Don't look so worried," he said with quiet assurance gently breaking his previous life as a mute. "Would you like to come through?" He said putting like law although it was a question. The man allowed Joseph to pass whereupon he shepherded him into the room of the clucking ladies.
"If you would like to take a seat," said Mrs Standard. "We have come to a decision. We would like to offer you the position of Teacher of English. Congratulations."
Joseph took a deep sigh of relief. A smile emerged from his face and he thanked the ladies for their decision.
"We were quite impressed," said Mrs Grouch. We're not always impressed are we Mrs Stand-ard?"
"No, we're not Mrs Grouch. You did very well Joseph," said Mrs Standard corroboratively and not without an air of superciliousness.

In truth, the two ladies felt quite pleased with themselves because the appointment of Joseph with the previous weeks recruitment of Ms Proper meant that the department had a full com-plement of staff and that would mean they would be under less pressure. Joseph felt grateful for the opportunity and thanked all those around. He shook hands and exchanged pleasant-ries before stepping out of the room with the round table and the chairs that had been posi-tioned around it.

As he was leaving, the Head Teacher, Mr A Differ, popped out of his office to perform the per-functory hand-shake and pat on the back. The interview had broken up and each person dis-appeared into the darker reaches of the school leaving Joseph alone and feeling vulnerable. He had forgotten the way out: the Head teacher pointed to him; his finger waving towards the door:
"There, that's the way out," he seemed to whisper. "Go…"
Feeling exposed, Joseph collected himself. He passed a flight of stairs leading to higher places and excited through the doors he had not long since entered.

Joseph had got himself into a position of responsibility and he was pleased. The fresh air in-vigorated him and he felt free again but he also felt strangely divorced from the success he had just earned. It was as if someone else had triumphed, that he indeed was not one person but two. There was one person who had to do the day to day things like everyone else and this person was the one that had just got the job. And then there was this other one who saw everything with an ironical aloofness; a person who now took over.

This other person knew that this other self had done well and done well in the eyes of others and that pleased him but he himself did not feel any genuine self-gratification. It was a feeling of self-worth that seemed to miss him because it belonged to the other him and the network of people who invented his other constructed version. They judged and judged according to standards which were not his.

He trundled back to his car and drove the short journey home. It was necessary to turn the wipers on as the drops of rain had gathered apace. As the rain pat patted on the car roof and windscreen, Joseph fell into a dreamy reverie. They had just invited him to work in their school but he felt abandoned; lost to the outside world with all its whims, disappointments and downpours. He needed external confirmation to be sure that what had just happened had just happened and so as he got out of his car and into his house, he rang his mother.

The news of his appointment was greeted with joy and kind words from his family but Joseph had mixed feelings. He saw possibilities but he was also anxious about starting his teaching career. Would he make the grade? Would the children respect him? Or would he find himself in trouble?

Chapter 2: The Year Ahead

The car park was full and signs of life were returning to the school now that the summer break was ending. A bird could be seen hopping from branch to branch on the old oak tree that stood inside the grounds between the main gates and the main entrance. The school felt eerie without the children; corridors were empty, classrooms lay dormant, there was no one to shout at or to get in a tizzy over. It was just the teachers who collected in the odd room here, the odd room there.

Mrs Grouch sat Joseph and Ms Proper down at her desk and gave them their timetables for the new school year which was due to start in earnest the following day. Today they were in for training purposes and with them being new teachers they had extra information to digest and take on board. Mrs Grouch liked to run a tight ship that was high on organisation, sched-ules, speadsheets, planning and foresight. Everything had to be in its place. Every aspect of teaching, planning, and implementation had to be in its box and be clearly visible and presented in an attractive manner. She wanted her staff to be clear upon how things were done.

And so was the scene all over the school; The Head, The Deputies, The Head's of Depart-ment, The Head's of Year, were getting their staff ready for the morning influx. Joseph and Ms Proper sat with their files, organisers and diaries at the ready:
"Now the yellow file is your key stage three file and the red one is for key stage four," said Mrs Grouch, "inside your files you will find your personal information, your timetable, the sanctions pyramid, departmental and staff meetings, your long, middle, and short term planning and the National Curriculum. Now you need

to ensure all preparation is completed and kept up to date," she instructed.

Mrs Grouch was in a fairly good mood because nobody had had time to make a mistake or fall behind in their work-load and duties. Mrs Grouch did have a sense of humour but unfortunately it was only allowed to surface if everything was ship-shape. If things fell out of place, if there was opacity, an anomaly or a question mark where there should be transparency, consistency and a full stop, she would become as unforgiving as Our Maker had been when He had given out her looks: "Now you need to make sure that you cover each aspect of the National Curriculum and show where you have done it in your planning," she continued.
Mrs Grouch was well past her best; she looked every year of her fifty-eight and perhaps a few more besides. She had little time for the twee and care-free for she had had to work hard in her life and she expected the same from everyone else in at least equal measure, and if that could add a wrinkle or a furrowed brow to the well turned-out, what could be better?
"You will need to set out each text type you will be doing for GCSE and ensure you cover the syllabus," she continued further.
Mrs Grouch had never been able to turn heads and what's more she had known that she never would from an early age. She had, however, been successful in many other respects: she had managed to find an upstanding husband and they had had a daughter who was doing very well. She had cemented herself into the position of Head of Department over the last half-dozen years and she had the guile and determination to hold onto the post for a few years yet.

Her Deputy, Ms Steal, was sniffing round, hoping to usurp her position in the fullness of time and Mrs Grouch had learnt to live with this irritation. Having been quick to see the threat, Mrs Grouch was even quicker to ensure that each of her new teachers knew their subordinate place:

"You will need to decide upon which texts you are going to use and you will need to make a record of how many you are using," she added.

Mrs Grouch had learnt over the years to out do people with her intellect and wit. The timetable she had handed down to Joseph and Ms Proper was designed to give them a manageable start, but more importantly it relieved her of the classes that were a strain on her sensibilities:

"Now Joseph and Ms Proper I have decided to give you classes across the age range of com-pulsory education but I have not given you any further educational classes because I don't want to burden you with Advanced Level responsibilities as well as Key Stage Three and Four." In truth, the Advanced Level pupils were the more mature pupils who could provide stimulating company and she wanted them for herself:

"I have decided to give you each two Year Seven English classes and a Year Seven form class, as the little ones are easiest to handle. They don't know what to expect so you will have space to find your own way and set down a marker. I'm going to give you the same set (set three out of four for joseph and set two for Ms Proper with set one being the brightest children and set four being a small class of slow learners) so you can halve the amount of preparation needed to be undertaken."

"Thank you. That's thoughtful; it will give us time to concentrate on other matters," said Ms Proper thinking about her private life. And so in one fell swoop the new teachers had taken four Year Seven classes; Mrs Grouch had long since grown tired of their youthful exuberance and so she could now wash her hands of them and forget about their trivial concerns altogether.

In Year Eight, Joseph was given the top set; Ms Proper did not teach Year Eight. Nothing re-markable there, no, Mrs Grouch's next moment of ingenuity surrounded Year Nine Study Skills. Ms Proper instead had a Year Nine English class and a Study Skills class whereas Joseph had a Study Skills class only. Study Skills was a non-curriculum subject which teachers and pupils treated with disdain and ran from like the plague. It was taken once a week in the computer suite in middle school:
"I'll give you each a Study Skills class because that will give you a chance to work in the com-puter suite; we need to develop our information technology skills so you two young sparks can be at the forefront of the endeavour," she said. "Us old ones, we know how to turn them on but that's about it," she lied as she was computer literate.

Between the two new teachers, Mrs Grouch had managed to wash her hands of Year Seven (there was nothing she could do about Year Eight) and Study Skills; the subject that no one wanted to look at or cared for. Now for Key Stage Four. In Year Ten and Eleven, girls dreamt of boys and boys noticed girls. Mrs Grouch noticed the boys noticing the girls and the girls noticing being noticed by the boys and remembered how she had not been noticed with any favour as a young girl at school.

In her infinite wisdom, Mrs Grouch on her succession to Head of Department decided that it would be much the best if the boys were separated from the girls at Key Stage four. Now we can't have any adolescent romances when pupils ought to be paying attention to their text books now can we? Mrs Grouch had a Masters in Education to prove that we can't and so

Year Ten and Eleven were taught in single sex classes.

"Right Joseph, I am going to give you Year Ten and Eleven set two girls. Again, the same set, this will cut down the amount of preparation. And Ms Proper, I'm giving you the Year Ten set three girls and in Year Eleven you can have the boy's remedial class. It's only a small class and they won't give you much marking to do."

Mrs Grouch didn't care much for pretty youthful looking girls, when she saw them she saw herself as a girl and felt resentful, boys were less conniving and the more sophisticated ones could be quite a pleasure to sit with. So she employed her sense of cunning to contrive the classes of her choice all the while having the wit to maintain that she was doing Joseph and Ms Proper a favour.

So she had got rid of the little ones, Study Skills and the girls at Key Stage four. What a coup. And she even managed to prise thanks (as Ms Proper was thinking of her private life and Jo-seph was eager to please) for it and pass herself off as a thoughtful do-gooder. With that all sorted it was now time for a cup of tea and a gossip in the staffroom.

Chapter 3: first steps

The first day of the new school year arrived; noise filled the corridors as excited children met friends who they had not seen for six weeks. Staff and children who had attended the previous year went this way and that with the assurance that a familiar environment brings. The hustle and bustle of staff and children alike falling over each other, pushing to get to their classrooms, intimidated Joseph.

He walked amongst them with unease; they walked in groups, they knew who their friends were and they knew where they were going. The pupils looked at Joseph and he felt vulnera-ble; he was unsure of his fate just like the fresh intake making the transition from primary school. Both he and they were unsure about where they should be going and how they were going to be treated once they got to where they did not know where they were going.

Joseph pushed his way passed the pupils; he exited upper school in the direction of lower school. He was due to meet his new Year Seven form class; he was required to take them for registration and take them through the rules and procedures that outline the behaviour of pu-pils at the school. Ms Proper set off in the direction of middle school to meet her form class to do likewise.

When Joseph arrived at his form room door, his form class was lined up outside along the cor-ridor wall. They were all neatly dressed in their uniform and looking-up apprehensively about what was to come. Joseph opened the door and in they all went. They each chose a seat, sat down and looked up awaiting instruction.

"Right, this morning, what we are going to be doing is going through the rules of the school, the procedures and how we expect you to behave whilst you are here, but first of all I will take the register to see who is here," said Joseph.

As Joseph began to call the different names the rhythmic monotony of the name followed by "Sir" took over him. He suddenly felt like he was eleven again but he had the physical appearance of a man so he couldn't have been. He was nevertheless taken back; he remembered being one of them but then there was a thick black line, a darkness that spread in between him now the teacher and him then; the small boy who had looked for guidance and leadership…

Joseph had no real story of his own or if he had it was one of shyness, losing his way, loneli-ness anxiety and pain. Darkness had descended and life had passed him by. He had no no-tion of the illness which had shown signs of life at 17 and at present lay bubbling under the surface and so he remained blissfully ignorant and strangely warm hearted towards his fellow man who had actually taken advantage of him on many occasions.

In consequence of the condition, Joseph had no real grip on the world, he had no fixed ideas about how others should behave; he was a space; he was a blank piece of paper upon which the pupils could write their stories and he could create one of his own. As he called out the last name and put down the red diagonal mark, he looked up and felt empathy. He, like they, were vulnerable; he too was waiting for guidance and in an uncanny sense they mirrored each other's position in life more than any of them could have supposed.

Meanwhile in middle school, Ms Proper was giving form class instructions before they entered the classroom:
"Can you listen very carefully please? Thank you. Now in a moment I am going to let you in the classroom. When you enter the classroom I would like you to sit boy-girl-boy-girl. I want you to remember where you are sitting. I will be writing down your name on a seating plan of the classroom so that I know who you are and where you should be. I want you to sit in your chosen seat permanently. Do not change your seating position or I will not know who you are. Okay, in you go sitting boy-girl-boy-girl," said Ms Proper opening the door for the first pupil and shutting it behind the last.

As Ms Proper stood at the front of the class and welcomed her children she remembered when she was that high and thought of all the enjoyable experiences she had had between then and now. Ms Proper had her own story which quite rightly left space only for similar compatible stories from people of her standing.

Ms Proper's first steps had been greeted with joy by her family. Her first steps, her first words, her first day at school, primary and secondary, her first boy-friend, it had all been a time of pleasure. She had had an enjoyable life so far that had provided satisfaction if nothing particularly far from the ordinary. Her story was one which she kept to herself in the classroom; the children were not entitled to pry and she was not going to allow the space left with the absence of her story be filled by any of their little tales or intrigues. They were there to learn and that was mostly all. Anecdotes that are unmistakably childlike and could be re-counted in the staffroom for the amusement of her colleagues were good but that was as far as it went.

As Ms Proper finished off the register and finished off the seating plan; she started on the use of the journal: "The journal is this small little red book which will keep you organised and well behaved. In the journal you will find your timetable and you will find each page is like a diary. Each school day is set out with each week taking up a double page. Now each entry is to record your homework and any useful information. Each night you must get a parent to sign your journal. Now this is how we monitor you. If you have done really well, a teacher may put a credit in your journal which, if you get enough, you will be rewarded with a certificate. If however you have been naughty, the teacher will use your journal to report misbehaviour which will be seen by me, who you will need to answer to, and of course your parents will see it also as they will be signing your journal each night. There is no getting out of the system. This is the way we operate at this school and it is a condition of you place here," concluded Ms Proper as the bell sounded for the next period.

With that, classrooms emptied and corridors became congested. Kids fell over each other in the quest for the next nugget of learning. Teachers squirmed in amongst them and the poor little Year Sevens got caught up and buffeted here there and everywhere. Joseph and Ms Proper sent their form class onto their next lesson where they would meet another new teacher whilst they faced up to the task of meeting their classes.

The school buildings were shaped in a triangular formation; it was divided into three parts: up-per, middle and lower school. Joseph's teaching classroom was upper school. Upper school was shaped like a crucifix; formed by a long vertical corridor and a shorter horizontal one. The top end of the cross housed the senior management offices, staff toilets and a small chapel. The long corridor below the cross had a number of doors leading to classrooms; then there was the intersection where each corridor met and formed a small concourse.

The concourse was a place where pupils would loiter and teachers would supervise. The shorter horizontal corridors led to the main hall at one end and to the technology rooms at the other end, and then, back in the concourse, laid a set of double doors leading to the staffroom and adjacent a flight of stairs led to higher places.

Joseph found his classroom up the stairs and he took to it like a mistreated orphan boy hap-pening upon a loving mother. It was a haven from the rough and tumble of pupils falling over each other in pursuit of their classroom for next lesson. Whilst it provided Joseph with sanctuary, it took him a while to make it characteristically his classroom. There was history in that classroom; a history that did not belong to him but invaded his consciousness refusing to leave like a ghost forever haunting it long lost castle.

Old teachers and old pupils had been through that classroom. People he did not know and would not know. He did, however, hear their distant cries. It was only a matter of chance that they were not going to be sitting in front of him next period. There were old work books and piles of goodness knows what towering up from the floor like historical monuments standing as evidence of an industrious past. Children screaming and adults going mad. He could not just throw them away; they might still be breathing; voices of anguish might still be heard; so there they stood, firm, solid, secure of their immediate future.

The chairs and tables remained as they were found and no new work appeared upon the wall for some time. He did not yet feel entitled to paper over the past and muffle those last remain-ing cries that had not yet died. Joseph was hesitant; he found it difficult to impose himself; he was new; he needed time to settle in.

Chapter 4: A Different Culture

St Mary's was Roman Catholic in persuasion; prayers and bible study were all part of the course and there was religious symbolism to be found throughout the school. The children did not like Religious Studies much but the word of the Lord played a significant part in their thinking and the majority, whilst not necessarily being regular church goers, retained their faith long after their time here.

Their parents wanted them to have a Catholic upbringing and many of the pupils when they had grown up, left, found a playmate and cavorted at their leisure, decided to give their chil-dren a Catholic education. The parents and the children were broadly speaking middle-class. They were privileged and the majority were brought up in a law obeying environment that placed value on good manners and courtesy.

Ms Proper fitted in well with the ethos of the school, whilst lacking piety, she had a middle class outlook and she had fixed ideas about how the start of her career was going to be and she was prepared to stamp her authority on matters relating to her from the outset. Her teach-ing room was situated in middle school which was rectangular in shape; it had two floors and it consisted of just the one long corridor with classrooms running off either side. She walked purposefully half way down the corridor and turned into her classroom.

Everything was in its place; the white-board, the over-head projector, the display area, the chairs and tables were neatly arranged and she had the various other bits of teaching para-phernalia that would provide the oil for an educationally smooth running engine, in place and ready at her disposal. She had cleared out the rubbish, the obsolete, and all that could have been useful to someone at some point, ready for the new term. She knew what she wanted and she was able to remove any remnants from the past which might try to interfere with her here, now, and in the future.

And with that she left her classroom for the staffroom, happy that she was ready to join the brood that was the English department. She was confident that she was going to fit in com-fortably and make her own mark. Ms Proper walked over towards upper school with a steady posture and presence despite being fairly short in height. She knew which way she was going, she had it all worked out in her mind, the staffroom was right then left and she had ear-marked a comfortable seat for herself amongst the English clan.

She sat down in the comfortable seat that she had reserved for herself and glanced around the staffroom with an air of contentment and expectation. What could she do whilst she waited for her colleagues to arrive? She looked down into her bag and viewed her immaculately kept registers, records and diary. No, they were already; there was nothing to add. Again she looked around the staffroom and saw her cup sat on the draining board. She had selected it from her kitchen and placed it on the draining board during the summer holiday ready for break-time in the coming school year.

She jumped up and took bold strides towards the kettle. She picked it up, filled it and set it to boil; with that she had passed her first initiation test into the English department. Just as the kettle was coming to the boil, the nucleus of the department appeared on the scene:
"Look at this Mrs Standard," said Mrs Grouch, "Ms Proper's going to do very well here; look she's well

trained," she said pointing at the cups that were now lined up for filling:
"And have we got some chocolates there? Said Mrs Standard expectantly.
Ms Proper looked at her with surprise:
"Well I can give her marks out of ten for the tea making but she is definitely going to lose out in the chocolate biscuit category," said Mrs Standard with characteristic gusto.
Ms Proper felt relief when she realised that Mrs Standard was playing with her: "So I should remember the chocolate biscuits," she said buying into the joke.
"And if you could get some of those nice little strawberry slices, oooh there is nothing like those strawberry slices," chipped in Mrs Grouch.
They sat down with their tea and gradually other teachers from other departments began to swell the numbers until the staffroom was buzzing with the same excitement as the concourse which was by now packed with pupils ready to begin their day.

Joseph descended the stairs and snuck into the staffroom as the bell sounded. The shrill ring had the effect of precipitating a gradual hush until all the teachers had been silenced:
"Morning everybody," said Mr A Differ, "Well, a week into the first term back and it already feels like a life time (twitters of amusement could be heard). I want to place special emphasis on behaviour; some pupils don't seem to be getting back into the routine as I would like. If you do see any untoward behaviour please stamp it out as quickly as possible. I am placing special emphasis on this because an unfortunate incident occurred on Friday which has led to our first suspension of the year which inside of a week must be a record. Mrs Standard has dealt with the incident so do you want to come in here?" said Mr A Differ to Mrs Standard.

"As Mr A Differ has told you, there was an incident on Friday which has caused much alarm. Heather Firk came into school with a lighter and she was going around lighting other pupil's hair. Of course this could have been most serious; thankfully no real damage has been done. Heather has now been suspended; I spoke to her mother but she does not seem able to control Heather but it has been agreed that she is not to come into school this week. She will be staying at home; if you do teach Heather can you please give me any work that she could be doing and we will have it sent to her, thank you." Said Mrs Standard.

"To reiterate then, I don't want incidents such as these to come the norm so if we can get roll-ing as quick as possible, get the pupils into classrooms, get them settled down to the work ahead and make sure that they aren't allowed to slip into bad habits. If we can do this, we will be starting on the right track, and starting as we means to go on which I think is important. So if we can all do that it would be of great benefit as we all do need to work as a team to ensure there are no weak links in the system, as it were; providing we can work as one we should be able to cut out any wayward behaviour before it starts. I would appreciate your support and I think now that we all understand why we do have a hair-spray ban. These rules that we have are important and it is equally important that we enforce them. Mrs Faith…"

"Thank you, morning everybody, as we move into our second week of our new year, I thought in this morning's prayer we could properly welcome the new staff into our community and I thought we might consider the role of the stranger and how we regard outsiders in our communities. Thinking over the last week, have we invited them with open arms into our community or have we been distant and perhaps even cold? Dear Lord, at a time when we are welcoming new staff and pupils to our school community, give us

the strength to hold out the hand of friendship and resist the temptation of turning our backs. Give us the strength of understanding and the strength to consider those who might not have the warmth and security of belonging to a community. Today, on this first day of the second week of the school year, lets us pull together and unite as one so that we can go forward and be stronger and represent your values of love and forgiveness, in the name of the Lord, Amen," said Mrs Faith dipping and rising as appropriate.
"Amen," they said in unison.
And with that the first morning briefing of the second week was over. Teachers finished their conversations, said hello to those they had missed as they got up to check the cover-board and exited the staffroom into the concourse and on to their registration rooms.

Chapter 5: Different files

Ms Proper was well versed in teaching procedures and was used to children in a way that Jo-seph needed to learn. She had expectations that she insisted would be met and she would not be compromising. The first few days and weeks of her teaching were characterised by the implementation of tried and tested methods. When the children came into the class she waited until they were quiet and would not start until they were listening. The register would be called, the lesson would commence and if any pupil failed to live up to her standards they would receive a black mark in their journal which had to be signed each night by a parent.

She knew about putting the aims and objectives on the board; she instinctively put down the date, the title and numbered each stage of the work to be tackled. The work was attractively presented, clear, and stylishly written and underlined in the important places. It was not long before her walls were adorned with newly produced work.

Joseph meanwhile was a living breathing example of unpreparedness. The truth was that he was unfamiliar with the school routine and he had lived a life since his own childhood far re-moved from children and the school work place. Not only this, but his other self had emerged at the time of transition from primary school to secondary. This other self had taken him further and further from reality. This left him ill prepared for many of the practical hurdles that were up and coming.

His practice year had been far from rigorous; he had managed to stumble his way through but he was still without many of the useful habits synonymous with teachers and effective teach-ing. Joseph would forget to do the most elementary requirements such as taking the register, "I want to know where you are and who you are with. You must be back before it gets dark. No you may not go out! You must not tell anyone about this…" he heard from a pile of books threatening to collapse. At first his lessons lacked the ordinary structure to be found in other classrooms. He seemed to have no rules or regulated procedure to follow.

Ms Proper would automatically follow the set protocol but Joseph would forget to put the date on the board perhaps because he simply would not see it as necessary or maybe it was be-cause he did not know what day it was; there often was no title and seldom ever was it under-lined if it did appear.

As Mrs Grouch had predicted, the Year Seven were easy to control at the beginning. They were too scared of getting into trouble and so they would sit quietly and await instruction. As time passed, however, they lost their self-consciousness and as Mrs Grouch well knew, they became tiresome in their spiritual zeal. Mrs Grouch expected both Joseph and Ms Proper to control any exuberant behaviour and ensure the English Department maintained its reputation as a department of high standards.

Joseph was required to meet his buddy each week to show that he was coping with the de-mands of the job. Mrs Putton was assigned to Joseph. She herself found it difficult to cope with all the work load. Being catholic she had a number of children, accommodating her family and working full time and being in charge of Key Stage Three was an impossible task that she somehow managed:
"Right then Joseph, I need to see your Key Stage Three and Four files," said Mrs Putton.

"Okay," said Joseph, "but where are they he thought to himself. Were they upstairs or were they in his bag in the staffroom?"

He stepped out of Mrs Putton's classroom and into the staffroom. He had a rummage in his bag but no there was nothing to be found. Feeling slightly panicked he stepped out of the staffroom and up the stairs. He went into his classroom and looked through his filing cabinets:

"Thank God," he thought to himself, there they were, the yellow and red files. He picked them up and scampered down to Mrs Putton's classroom which was directly below:

"Right let's have a look through these," said Mrs Putton with no time to waste. It was nearing the end of the day and she was already thinking about picking the kids up, putting on the din-ner, doing some marking and then putting on a wash:

"Right, Key Stage Three, where's your overview?"
"Overview?" said Joseph absent-mindedly.
"Yes; you should have an overview which sets out each area of the National Curriculum and determines which week and which lesson you are going to teach it in,"
"I don't think I've done that," said Joseph slightly perplexed.

Mrs Putton did not say anything but the words, "bloody hell, what have we got here," went through her mind.
"Look this is your overview here, this is the National Curriculum for this term. They correspond. You need to set out the different things you are going to teach on it.

"What about you're planning, let's have a look at that. I would like to see your forward planning for years seven, eight, ten and eleven," said Mrs Putton as she flicked impatiently through the file.

"Right, lets have a look. I can see that you've got planning done up to now but where's the forward planning?" Asked Mrs Putton.
"Well, I'm just about to do it," said Joseph fearing the worst.
"You need to have at least a week's worth of planning done ahead," said Mrs Putton.
"Arhhh right," said Joseph. A week ahead. Mrs Putton had no idea that Joseph was many years behind. The disparities beween Joseph's past and present realities were beginning to come into view. He hadn't kept up with his peers and in some respect he was playing catch up and when he was ask to produce material for the future he was found lacking.

Meanwhile in middle-school, Ms Proper was going through the exact same scenario with Ms Steal except of course the results. Ms Proper had her files at the ready, the yellow one on top of the red. She opened up the yellow one and inside lay her overview and planning. It was ordered, neatly set out and crystal clear; it said in a loud resounding voice, that this teacher, Ms Proper, had her life in order, her career in hand, and her future ready to be enjoyed.
"Well that's fine," said Ms Steal hoping that Mrs Grouch would not long be for this world. "Yes, you've got you're planning all in order, everything seems to be ship-shape, next week we'll look at some marking and some marking schemes okay?"
"Yes," said Ms Proper feeling pleased.
Back in upper school, Mrs Putton, found that she was buddy to a new teacher who wasn't particularly organised. She would have to speak to Mrs Grouch because Mrs Grouch liked to run a tight ship and this would not do and she had her own life to contend with. She would need to be out the door in a few minutes, racing off down the road in her people carrier in search of her children who need picking-up.

She would need to speak to Mrs Grouch, she could deal with it and with that the bell sounded. Joseph was left with his files all back to front and higgle de piggle de. Mrs Putton was out the door, the sound of chairs going up on tables and kids escaping the repression of the classroom reverberated around the school and Heather Firk sat at home for she had been suspended.

Like Ms Proper, Joseph had been given two files and a diary to keep him organised. Joseph however failed to impose order on his paper. Mrs Grouch would need to give him maternal grump of dissatisfaction and tell him to get his house in order. Having spoken with Mrs Putton, Mrs Grouch sat Joseph down in her office the next day and asked him to show her his lesson plans: "Arhhh, lesson plans, yes, hmm, I'll just go and get them." He stepped out of the office through Mrs Grouch's classroom and into his own which lay beside it. They were in one of his files. Which one? He turned around and returned to Mrs Grouch who was sat expectantly waiting for him:
"In here, are they?" She said taking the red file. She opened it and lots of bits of paper fell to the floor. "O my God," she said, "tell me these are not your lesson plans, what have we got here?" she said leaning over and picking up scraps of paper. Joseph knelt to the ground and gathered the last remaining plans that he had done.
"This is the work I've been doing with…"
"But these should be on the planners in your file; they should be set out like a diary so you know what you're doing from day to day and where you are going. They should provide you with support and keep you on track and should be neatly arranged if possible.
"arhh right," said Joseph feeling a let-down.
"You are going to need to transfer these lesson plans onto the proper planner. Some of the work you have

got on here looks quite good, but it needs to be organised," she continued.

Mrs Grouch got out the proper organisers and planners and proceeded to show Joseph how it ought to be done. Mrs Grouch liked men who had a helpless quality to their character and so, whilst she was not pleased, she sent Joseph on his way in the hope that he would now pull his socks up.

Chapter 6: Troublesome Children

In time Joseph found his two Year Seven teaching classes contained children prone to misbehave, the Year Eight contained children who were clever enough to challenge intellectually, the Year Nine class contained children who did not know how to behave; partly because their bodies were developing an outwardly adult appearance yet they still had childish enthusiasm and openness; the two coupled together produced an irreverence to drive any respectable person up against the wall. The Year Ten class needed GCSE results and the Year Elevens needed results urgently but did not have the enthusiasm of Year Ten to attain them.

For Ms Proper, the two Year Seven classes contained children more able and less likely to play-up. Her Year Nine English class and Study Skills class contained children who needed a close eye keeping on them. Her Year Ten girls could at times be quite spiteful and her Year Eleven boys were in many senses easy; they had few expectations, they produced little work to mark and they thought she was quite good looking for a teacher so they deferred to her aura most of the time. They could at times be uncouth and lazy but it was their loss not hers.

In the same way that Joseph failed to impose order on his paper-work, he did not impose the law in the classroom or if he did it was malleable. He looked at the hand he was dealt, accept-ed it, and looked to improve it as the game unfolded. He did not set a standard which the chil-dren had to reach. Dealing with the needs of the classes and the individual pupils within those classes was a tiring experience but it was one that Joseph and Ms Proper took seriously. Ms

Proper however had a much different approach and style to Joseph.

Ms Proper began to shape her classes to her standards in line with her own story but Joseph seemed to wait to find out what shape they were before shaping because he did not have a story. Ms Proper would pick up on inappropriate behaviour and squash it from the start, Jo-seph would often miss it at the beginning but when he saw it he would also wonder where it came from and in so doing he began to weave his own story which was inextricably linked to theirs.

The stories of the children in his classes were active stories; imaginative stories, stories which spoke of innocent adventure, there was friendship, love and magical wizards and witches. And then there were the cruel stories; ones that spoke of hatred, betrayal and then, and then, there wasn't a story, a story that did not speak at all.

Joseph would listen to all their stories; he bore all this by himself. The story did not and did matter completely. Regardless, the stories etched themselves upon Joseph's face over the year; he walked in and out of each classroom across the school, a wide expanse, hiding and showing and giving.

It took Joseph time to acclimatise to his role as teacher. The pupils would bring their little lives up the stairs to Joseph's classroom where he would need to fit them into his lessons. The children were not excluded by him despite what problems they might bring into the school with them. The children therefore felt able to express themselves whether it was inappropriate or entirely necessary. Freedom was good and bad. It could be used destructively but it

gave Joseph an insight that Mrs Standard did not want to look at and would not tolerate:
"The cleaners deal with the dirt and I'm not a cleaner, I'm a teacher," she said with all the as-surance and maternal love that wells up inside a woman over nine months of kicking and nourishment theft.

Ms Proper had always worked according to the law and she therefore found its implementation much easier. Ms Proper had her children trained according to her rules. They perhaps did not like it but they each knew their place and what was expected from them. They each had to sit according to the seating plan and they each had to show common courtesy and behave according to classroom etiquette. They could not just call out, they could not wander around the room but they were to sit still and talk only when given permission about the task they had been set. And so the beginning for the children in the classes of Joseph and Ms Proper were quite different.

Up the stairs in upper-school, Joseph sought to control his classes; he was playing catch-up; without the necessary parameters to contain behaviour in place from the beginning, the chil-dren had exploited the lack of boundaries and expressed themselves in new ways; sometimes disruptive, sometimes imaginatively.

Each class brought its own challenges for both Joseph and Ms Proper. For Joseph, the form class was in many ways quite demanding as it turned out because many of the children came from broken homes. Homes where mum hated dad, dad hated mum or someone had died or some stranger was living in the house. It wasn't ideal but these things happen and it's better to come from a broken home than a rock solid home that delighted in the devil's work. Joseph was pleased to be given such a class because he knew what it was like. Ms Proper's form class had no such problems.

With the Year Sevens being new, Joseph could learn with them. The other classes however had stolen a march on him. Now the Year Sevens were beginning to forget that they were new and the Year Elevens were having to face up to the impending mock exams. The Autumn term was in full swing, the hour had gone back and the dark nights were approaching. The wind was gusting up and the children were being blown around in the playground. The old oak tree was vainly hanging onto its leaves and hats and scarves were becoming common sight.

Often Joseph could not get the children to act as he would like them to because some of them would interrupt him or he would not know what to say next. When one child seemed to get away with interrupting him, some of the others would see that it was not only acceptable but advantageous as one could gain attention and currency which could be used to pay for privi-lege. I'll have your pen, I'll take your seat, I'm talking, do you mind?

Some children began to dominate, the reading was not shared out, some children had a bigger say than others and it was these powerful children that began to set the rules. Joseph did not know how to treat children; he was learning but it took time and in that time some children took advantage. He was too concerned about the work and he did not see (although the signs were there) that discipline needed to come first. One could explain the intricacies of life and literature but if nobodies listening; what's the point? Once discipline has been established the work could follow. Discipline first, work second. It took time for Joseph to learn this and whilst he did the powerful children filled the space he left. How to get that discipline? Now that's the question.

Whilst Joseph had surrended territory, he found out what life was like in the land of trouble-some children. He found out which children were likely to bully him, behave in an inappropri-ate fashion, what the inappropriate behaviour constituted and who were keen to work through their own volition. A glimpse into the lives of children without rules gave him a glimpse into their home-life. The door had opened to a stranger.

Since Joseph had ceded ground to pupils in his class; the most troublesome pupils had a head start upon him. They had set a precedent; they had gotten away with naughty behaviour and they expected to be able to at their own discretion. They had grown bold where Joseph had started hesitant.

Fred Eades was probably his most difficult pupil in Year Seven. He was magnetically drawn to the life of lawlessness. He depended upon rules and knew them inside out but he had an irrestible desire to unburden himself from the shackles of law and order and then instantly regret it once he had intoxicated himself on the drug of weightlessness. And then he would go bright red angry looking at anyone who would attempt to admonish his behaviour.

Joseph was learning: he asked the children to listen; he asked them to be quiet so that they could hear his instructions and begin work. It took time because the children did not fear him. They knew he could be quite gentle and kind. They knew that he had patience and that they would not be cruelly reduced to pieces like one of those unlucky children savaged by a dog that you hear about in the tabloids from time to time. So each in their turn, he would ask them if they would listen and stop fiddling with this or that. They complied in time but it was an effort.

Fred was starting to get agitated. His time was nigh. Most of his fellow class-mates were ready and listening. Anticipation was heavy in the air. Joseph was onto disciplinary action if anyone talked:
"I have asked you several times to listen now. The next person to interrupt will be getting a warning in their journal."
Fred already had a number of warnings. He had the most in the year. Another one would get him into serious trouble and would mark him out as a trouble-making distinction. And so, when everyone was quiet and nobody else had the nerve to interrupt, Fred carefully, timing his act to perfection, lent back on his chair, in glorious isolation, not a care in the world, lent back on his chair, and when at approximately forty-five degrees he threw a pen up in the air, perpendicular to the table, smile a plenty, down it came, "weee," he called, caught it! 9.8, 9.7, 9.9, 9.7 & 9.7, rang out the judges…

Joseph was furious. How dare he undermine his hard work? He had striven to achieve an atmosphere where work could take place and this little upstart had blown it all away in a moment of gay abandonment:
"Who on earth do you think you are?" bellowed Joseph. "How dare you behave in such a manner? Do you think you are the exception to the rule? That you can behave in anyway you see fit? Do you."
Fred's demeanour had undergone a radical change. No longer was there that look of gay abandonment but now a look of bottled anger. It was as if the two faces belonged to different heads such was their immediate change. No residue lingered from that naughty boy

that ex-isted before but instead a boy who felt grievously wronged.
"No Sir," replied Fred ashamed of his own conduct.
"Journal on my desk now!"
And up got up with deep regret and grave misgivings with the system.
"Right, we'll try again…"

Mike Pico, a dark tanned boy, in the other Year Seven set demanded attention and he had leant every trick in the book designed to procure the concern of others. He did not fear adults; not even Mrs Satndard intimidated him. He would march around the school with the self-assurance of top dog. He wanted everything and was quite happy to kick and shout in order to get it. He called out, he waved his hand, he wrote on the table, he left a mess under his desk, he poked people, he stole, he lied, he sulked, he moaned, he buried his head with a stubbornness unsurpassed.

He never, however, exposed himself. He would commit crime after crime after crime with a sense of cunning resembling a wisely old fox or a dissembling cub. He would be embroiled in trouble-making but he would hide the fact and defend himself like no other to ensure he came out of any situation smelling like roses. He broke the rules but always under the cover of darkness and then he would use the rules to seek advantage and protection from the naïve and unsuspecting. He wanted to be involved; he wanted everything, accept, accept that exposure. Mike feared the world that Rees was irresistibly drawn to. He would rather bring everyone down than admit that he had transgressed the rules.

The Year Eights were challenging intellectually despite their age. What's age got to do with quickness of thought? Joseph had experience which can bring knowledge but it can also bring obstacles of learning. B goes after A and then C but why? There is no rhyme or reason but the bright children of Year Eight had no cause to change what they could follow naturally and with ease. They had no obstacles. In their young lives they had only known success and, for a few, it marred their character. Joseph was of humble roots; these children were privileged. A select band of individuals bullied Joseph because he would forget to put the date on the board, or he would not know what to say next, or his pronunciation would be awkward and betray and unfamiliar accent. "There is no room for you here," they would say with their warm houses and guardians of law and order.

How could they respect a man who spoke thus? What right did he have to teach them? Who teaches who? Yoda. Do Ya? Well lets have it you wrinkly old shit. And so the teacher and the disciple fought the perennial battle for knowledge; each fishing for the answer, each smelling a rat, and each enjoying the ride.

Joseph did not teach English to Year Nine. He taught Study Skills: the subject that nobody else wanted, the subject which no other teacher would touch. It was put upon Joseph and he had to bear with it. It was a subject that was directionless because it wasn't formally assessed and it was done on the computers and computers were not his thing.

Their bodies were changing; particularly the boys. Hair was growing in their pants and under their arm-pits. Their voices were breaking and their dicks were getting hard. The girls watched with eager anticipation, their breasts were already swollen and they had long since grown pussy hair and dropped blood from their knickers which were for some, now G-strings.

Whilst the Year Nine boys tried out the new toy that hung between their hairy legs and projected like a tank-gun, the girls shortened their skirts and slapped on their make-up. Whilst the boys underwent metamorphosis and the girls watched with interest, Mrs Grouch decided that it would be much the best if the boys were separated from the girls. Now we can't have children feeling horny in the classroom now can we? Mrs Grouch had a masters to prove we can't and so Year Ten and Eleven were taught in single sex classes. Hormones danced around the classroom. Year Ten and especially Year Eleven heaved. Hidden desire manifested itself in sweet-talk, doodles, longing, looking, gazing, boys out enjoying physical education. O! I'll give you physical education baby! Jokes were good. Who could be the naughtiest? Joseph, the girls? The girls, Joseph?
"Have you got a girl-friend?" said Emma Bylaw.
"Sort of x really," said Joseph lying for he had been unsuccessful with woman for many a year but he wanted a story to tell."
"What do you mean?" Enquired Emma.
"We've split. She wants children and I don't," admitted Joseph lying again.
"Why don't you want children? Asked Emma for she could not imagine going through life without a family.
"I'm not ready for the responsibility," said Joseph truthfully lying.
"You're sure you're not gay?" Teased Emma.
"Sure," said Joseph.
"What size shoe do you take?" said Emma pushing it.
"What exactly are you trying to work out?" Replied Joseph unimpressed.
"Have you ever had an affair with a pupil?" Asked Emma casually.
"No I have not," said Joseph resolutely.

The questions rained in and whilst the rain can be irritating it can also freshen the mind and liven the spirit. It moistens the bushes and makes the birds sing. And well, everyone gets wet from time to time. Joseph felt discomfort but he liked a shower each morning.

But not everyone likes a shower each morning because some people are so dirty that they are unable to get clean. They're not dirty but they feel dirty and water does not wash away feel-ings and memories now does it? Whilst Joseph often felt intimidated and exhausted by the children he began to fear the children less and less and he grew accustomed to their ways. Meanwhile, Ms Proper held discipline in her class. No child questioned her sexuality or de-manded to know what she did on a Friday night. She was a closed book on an ordinary life. Life was far more peaceful in her classroom but she was learning a little too.

Chapter 7: You Set Your Standard

That morning, a deep frost had set in. Temperatures had plummeted and people setting out to work all over the country had found the need to use their de-icer for the first time in many months. Joseph was no exception. Being pushed for time he hurriedly sprayed copious amounts of de-icer to unlock his frozen car door. It wasn't easy for Joseph to heat-up that day but with some ready-break and a mug of tea he was beginning to show signs of warming to the task and day ahead.

Joseph was learning all the time. It was his first year, learning did take place in his classroom, it was a bit noisy at times, but he was there, struggling but coping. He had meetings to attend, work to do, lessons to give, lessons to prepare, marking to undertake and homework to set. There were checks: can we see your lesson plans? It is okay to observe a lesson? It's time to see your buddy. No, it was time to see Mrs Standard. It was her responsibility to care for the new staff and ensure that their needs were being met and so he went to see her once a fortnight.

With Joseph's tutor classroom being in lower school, and his teaching room in upper school, he was required twice daily to make the trek there and back for morning and afternoon regis-tration. Mrs Standard faced the opposite situation. Her cosy little office was situated in the senior management area whereas her teaching room lay in lower school. They would there-fore pass each other on regular basis and exchange pleasantries.

Mrs Standard's office was positioned opposite the staff toilets and beside the Head Teacher's office. It was smaller than the Head Teacher's but still very cosy.

Joseph tapped on the door and poked his head around the door. At Mrs Standard's behest, he sat down on a red seat and gripped his file nervously:
"I won't be a minute Joseph," said Mrs Standard concentrating on less important things in life. Joseph sat patiently waiting.
"Arhhh yes. That's better. Eee," she said catching her breath. "Well now we need to arrange a lesson observation for your termly assessment. If we set a date this week, now what lesson would you like me to observe?"
Joseph considered. Now which lesson would be the easiest? He decided on the Year Seven class because they are the most easily duped. He could tell them that Mrs Standard, the Dep-uty Head, was coming in to see them (this in fact was her idea) and they must be on their best behaviour or else a monster would spring from the cupboard and eat them all up. He chose the right year group for such a method but the wrong period. The children were always more difficult to contain last thing in the afternoon. Nevertheless, the date had been set. The time was nigh. Mrs Standard was due to ascend the stairs and enter his classroom last period to-morrow.
 There was no free period. He was teaching every lesson that day. It would be all go and then Mrs Standard would be passing judgement on him at the end of the day. The Year Tens period one passed without comment, the Year Eights period two were bright, the first of his two Year Sevens were a contrast, the Year Nine's period four were a relief to wash your hands of, and then, dashing from one side of the school to the other, for Year Nine Study Skills was the exception as it was taught in the computer suite in middle-school, he reached his classroom to find Mrs Standard already there waiting for him.

Terrified. She frightened the life out of him. She sat at the back of the classroom with a pen and a clip-board. What poison was she going to spill over that page? Joseph had no struc-ture. Where was he to begin? At the start of course but where to next? Left? Right? Up? Down? Forward? Back? Follow that cab! The children were all lined up outside the class-room. Joseph had deceitfully told the children during afternoon registration that Mrs Standard would be in tomorrow's lesson to judge them and that they must line-up and behave through-out or she would be seriously angry. Joseph gave the children permission to enter and in they went, each in turn to their seat.

They all had a chosen place to sit but who would flourish and who would wilt. How would their lives develop. They each sat down; some were comfortable, some squirmed and Joseph just added to the agitation. Where were his board pens? What were they going to do? What's the fucking date? He composed himself. He did the register. Were they all there? Where is Sophie? Does it matter why she is absent? No, just as long as we have the absence recorded.
"Right! Today we are going to look at a piece of literature about the butterfly. Who can tell me something about butterflies? Yes Johnny."
"Their pretty and they change shape."
"Yes, that's right Johnny. What does he mean by change shape? Yes Chloe"
"Well Sir, he means that butterflies start off as caterpillars which are long and wiggly and then they go hard and crystallise. It's all sticky and messy but I think they have to do it."
"Yes, that's right Chloe."
"They only live for two seasons Sir. Like the hay Sir. It grows in the spring and then its har-vested by Autumn.

And it was at that point metamorphosis began to take place. The children changed; they forgot about Mrs Standard. They hadn't met Mrs Bylaw. They each found their own voice and Joseph found it difficult to keep them under wraps. They were not all listening. A few of them began to fiddle with their pens or anything discovered deep within their pencil cases. One or two started chatting. Joseph did not have command of their minds. He did not have control of their thoughts, opinions and decisions. They were free to form their own theories and explore a world where their own instinct and adventures were possible.

Mrs Standard had it all down. Johnny wasn't paying attention, Fanny was looking out of the window, Pete was calling out and Gemma was pushing Luke off his chair. It would all need to be discussed. Joseph needed to set his standard and enforce with all the power of the status quo that enshrined behaviour at St Mary's; vested interest; that was what was important and no, nothing must change the perennial cycle of missed opportunity.

"Thank you Year Seven for allowing me to come into your class and watch you working," she said knowingly. "It has been most enjoyable seeing you for myself. It's good to see what Year Seven are doing because I don't have a Year Seven class, she duped them. And so Joseph and Mrs Standard had led them up the garden path. Mrs Standard disappeared down stairs passed the brown seats and into her office that lay adjacent to the head, not as big but never-theless very comfortable.

She left the children in the dark, she abandoned them far, far down the garden path where lurked a snake. The bell suddenly sounded, "go, off you go," commanded Joseph. Mrs Standard was good at judging others: "You set your standard and the children rise to it or they are punished. It does not matter who the child is, boy, girl, black or white. It does not matter. Mrs Standard had it all down on her clip-board. Each different criticism had a number and each would need to be addressed in its turn. Joseph would need to rise to her standard and fulfil the different demands expected of a teacher. He would need more presence, more force and more awareness. The children needed to know that they were not free to do as they pleased but they must follow.

Chapter 8: Ms Proper

Ms Proper had erected her dainty little umbrella as a gentle shower fell from the skies. She was feeling fairly pleased with herself as her life was beginning to pan out as she imagined it. Mr Goodlife held open the door for her as she stepped into middle school: "Thank you," said Ms Proper looking up and smiling. "No problem," said Mr Goodlife, glancing back at Ms Proper's bottom and thinking what fun it would be if he was young again.
Ms Proper marched down the corridor and turned into her classroom. She put her bag down on her desk and took out the register and the materials she needed for the lesson soon to commence.

She sat down on her cushioned seat and viewed the neatly arranged work she had recently displayed on her walls. Her mind flittered from the lesson to come to the evening ahead. She was in a few moments to teach the art of reading between the lines to Year Nine but what dress was she to wear tonight more importantly? The green one or the blue one? What can you infer from a text without actually being able to identify it explicitly? The blue one would turn heads.

The bell rang to signal the end of break; they would be here soon. Her boyfriend, John, had proposed to her; she had the ring on her finger to legitimise their relationship. It flashed as she jiggled her finger; she could not but help notice the rays as they sent beams across her eye-line. The flashes of light dazzled in the sunlight that came in through the window. Each ray that penetrated her line of vision gave her a feeling of self-worth.

The Year Nines were due any moment; by now they were used to her ways. They were ex-pected to sit down at their desks in a sober fashion ready for work. And so in they came ready to start, careful not to cross the line that would get them into trouble. There was resistance and Heather Firk would still give Ms Proper a testing time but Ms Proper had her under the thumb and for the most part she was bearable.

Heather was prone to misbehave, she would want to get up out of her seat, she would use inappropriate language and she would hand in work that was poorly presented. Ms Proper had clamped down on her from the beginning. She gave Heather warnings in her journal, detentions, further disciplinary action from her Head of Year and she had driven home her point against Heather at parent's evening.
Parent's evening was Parent evening for Mrs Firk. She stepped into the school nervously. She hoped to say as little as possible and leave without delay:
"Goodevening," said Ms Proper, standing and shaking Mrs Firk's hand as they both sat down together.
"Evening," mouthed Mrs Firk half audibly.
"I'll get straight to the point Mrs Firk. Heather's behaviour, I will assume you know from the number of times I have had to write in her journal, is quite unacceptable. She can often find it difficult to settle, sometimes she takes no interest in the work and when she chooses not to work she distracts others which is not fair on the other children in the class."
"I know that she is difficult to handle. I have tried to talk to her but she does not seem to lis-ten," replied Mrs Firk.
"Well, if she does not change it is going to get serious. Decisions will shortly be made about what set she will be in next year and next year will be her GCSE year and the set she will be put in will contribute to the

decision about which paper she can take which will determine the grade she can achieve," said Ms Proper.
"I will talk to her again and try to persuade her to be a good girl," said Mrs Firk.
"It's in her best interest Mrs Firk," said Ms Proper. "It isn't too late to turn things around but it must start now."
"Of course, I will have a serious chat to her about her behaviour," said Mrs Firk reassuringly.
"Well I really do hope you can get through to her because it is such a shame to see a young person throwing away their chance in life," said Ms Proper,
"I think she just finds it difficult to concentrate just like her sister, I don't know where they get it from, I have tried with them really I have," returned Mrs Firk.
"I'm sure you have and it must be difficult," sympathised Ms Proper.
"It is, really it is. To have to go through this with one is bad enough but two, I am exhaust-ed,"complained Mrs Firk.
They looked up at each other and Ms Proper smiled sympathetically into Mrs Firk's imploring eyes all the while thinking "you weak woman."
"I don't know what to do next," added Mrs Firk.
"Well as long as we are aware of the situation and if we can just keep plugging away and re-minding Heather of the importance of good behaviour and doing well, I think we're doing the best we can," said Ms Proper fearful that she might be inviting Mrs Firk to unburden her trou-bles and break-downright there in front of her.
"Well, I will try, I certainly will try to get her to improve," said Mrs Firk.
"Okay, lets hope to see some improvement in the next term," concluded Ms Proper. And with that they each rose, thanked each other and Mrs Firk took herself off to the next teacher and Ms Proper prepared herself for the next parent.

Ms Proper had used each measure at her disposal and after sometime Heather was silenced as far as possible and Ms Proper could continue her teaching without undue interruption. Heather would enter the class with a sense of failure and resignation and accept the tyranny heaped up upon her. And so she sat down with her class-mates awaiting instruction: "Right class, today we're going to look at a piece of suggestive writing. Can you first of all read through the extract you have before you and list the number of possible reasons why the protagonist of the piece is reluctant to go home? I want you to read between the lines."
And so the class settled down to the task at hand and Ms Proper thought about the evening ahead, the green dress, yes, the green, and a flash of light beamed across her eye-line.

John held the door open for his fiancé, and he followed thinking what a cute arse she had and what a triumph it had been winning the rights to touching it. Their spirits were lifted by the wine they had drunk and the promising future that lay before them.
"Do you want a coffee dear?" Asked John who was in need of a sobering drink.
"Yes please," called out Ms Proper from the bedroom.
"Can you help me with my dress sweetheart?"
"Can I?" said John with a big smile on his face.
"Can you get the zip?"
"You look well sexy in this dress but even better without," said John with interest.
"Well, if you play your cards right and make that coffee by the time you're back I might have slipped into something a whole lot more comfortable, "said Ms Proper with an amorous appe-tite.

It was not long before the coffee cups stood half empty and the bed was rocking to and fro. Ms Proper lay on her back, legs spread wide apart. John had his penis up inside her. He held her right shoulder with his left hand and the top of her left leg with his right hand as he thrust in and out of her. She gripped his arse cheeks, pulling him in and out, willing him to find the right spot. A crucifix hung around Ms Proper's neck. It jumped each time john banged inside her. The coffee was splashing high up the sides of the cups and just as John ejaculated and Ms Proper let out a deep sigh of pleasure for the moment and a day well done, brown fluid spilt on each of the bedside cabinets.

John rolled over and took some deep breaths. He rolled the condom off his now limp penis, wrapped it up in a tissue and discarded it in the conveniently placed bin. The contents of the half-empty coffee cups came to rest and Ms Proper fell asleep safe in the arms of her fiancé who held her with appreciation because he did not like masturbating. She was a life-saver.

Chapter 9: Slow Growth and aberrant comments

The children had long since left the classroom, the dark clouds that had gathered up above began to disperse. Rays of light penetrated the wintry skies and sent beams of light into Jo-seph's classroom. Joseph had lied to the children. He purposely misled them in order to make his life easier. Mrs Standard had been complicit; she had descended the steps, disappeared into her cosy little office and buried her head in some matter concerning the respectability of the school and more specifically her position in that school and thought no more of it. She didn't see it as lying; she called it "psychology."

Up above the rays of light flickered intermittently as the wind blew the clouds hither and thither. The lesson observation hadn't been a disaster but there was plenty of room for improvement. The Deputy Head told Joseph that he must set the standard and insist the children met those requirements and with that she passed Joseph and he plodded on. She completed the paper-work; Joseph was free to move into the next term with fresh objectives.

Back in his classroom some children were beginning to wonder why Joseph did not maintain discipline and leadership like the other teachers, other kids revelled in the space Joseph had left. It was a space filled with unacceptable behaviour and humour. Joseph would see the funny side of indiscipline and it would take him longer to set about the work of the day. Chil-dren would chatter, they would fiddle with their pens, some would fail to do their homework and Joseph was slow to pick up on it. The children felt they had a reasonably good chance of getting away with misbehaving and if they did get caught they supposed Joseph would be lenient and perhaps even see the funny side. They would use the wrong type pen or write about taboo subjects. It was all good.

Joseph would be tripped up; he would be interrupted and ridiculed by some pupils. Joseph had allowed certain individuals to get away with unacceptable behaviour. In his class there were some children who were challenging his position and intimidating others. Rees and some of his mates were imposing their anarchic tendencies. Mike was dominating the reading. Amie was ridiculing, some of the Year Tens were too noisy, some of the Year Elevens were being explicit and the Year Nines... well that's another story.

It had to stop. Annie Friad would walk into the classroom with a sense of trepidation and wonder why Rees and his friends were allowed to make such a noise. Why were they allowed to interrupt, lean back on their chairs and chuck pencils case paraphernalia around the classroom? It was bad enough adjusting to the infinite problems of learning without receiving mixed messages from a teacher.

Barbara Square in Year Eight wondered how long Joseph would allow Amie to displace him as the leading light of the class. To what extent would he tolerate the ridicule she heaped upon him to the delight of her band of merry followers? In Year Ten, Celia Grade wanted to know why a small minority of girls were able to affect the teaching and spoil her chances of getting a higher mark. In Year Eleven, Bridget Fitch wanted to know why some girls could be so suggestive.

Where was Joseph? He needed to stand-up and dominate proceedings. He needed to force himself into their consciousness. They needed to feel his presence; a presence that would account for all of them, that would uplift them and inspire them onto better things. Had this been a difficult school he would have stood no chance, too much would have passed by. But this was a good school and he had a chance of clawing it back.

Joseph was determined to improve his classroom management. He was not going to let the children get the better of him. He was learning; like Ms Proper, he was beginning to automati-cally follow the set procedure. He would call the register, he would write the date on the board followed by the title and lesson objectives, and he would wait for the children to be quiet before he started. His past, present, inner-core and outer were beginning to collide and he felt some slight sense of wholeness for in his life he had lacked assertiveness but it was a necessity for this job.

There was, however, still a small minority misbehaving. He decided to go by the letter of the law. There was a sanctions policy operating in the school; he would enforce it and hope that it would yield the results that he desired. But then there was the work. The work took so much time and effort that he had little left over to devote to discipline. And then there was his character; he wasn't a tyrant, he wasn't interested in getting children into trouble, he found rule-breaking liberating, so how, how was he to condemn what he secretly admired?

He had to have discipline however. How to marry the two that was the question. Would good behaviour get into bed with freedom? Would they fornicate and produce a child called, "the ideal atmosphere for learning," for literature was a subject that looked at challenging the status que, the norms of society and freedom is a quality that many pursue whether it be from parents, peers or other figures of authority.

Discipline first and then learning. He needed to turn things around. He found that implementing the sanctions system with rigor did not work. If he became more challenging they resisted equally. He found that detentions meant that he lost his break but not only that; it was up to him to remember and it was up to him to chase after any absconders. This made his job more difficult rather than easier. The children began to see it as a challenge to engage in rather than back out of.

When the sanctions policy failed he discovered that listening, explaining and refusing to begin until his conditions were satisfied was the answer. It was not until he felt comfortable with his surroundings that he realised the power of silence. Wait. Refuse to start the lesson until the pupils were quiet, sitting up-right and listening. Do not set the work until these conditions were satisfied. This procedure worked in this school, not in many others but yes, in this, yes. Do not set the work until these conditions were satisfied. It took time but it was working. The children began to see that there were standards; that they did have to respect the teacher.

Joseph was beginning to gain a strangle hold on his classes but there was still a marked dif-ference between himself, Ms Proper and the rest of the teaching staff. Joseph did not patron-ise the children; he would listen and explain to them as an equal and he found that this created a special bond. Furthermore, Joseph had a unique sense of humour. His growth in his own psychology had been hindered since the transition between primary and secondary school; so in many ways he was on their level, whilst looking much older, he in some respects was actually the youngest in the class despite having the most miles on the clock by some way. Joseph had thought that some kids were just trouble, just like he was just a bit aloof but now he was beginning to see cause and effect behind behaviour.

Whilst he was now demanding certain standards of behaviour he would joke with the children. His classes would ask him personal questions. They would want to know his story. He would answer unlike Ms Proper as he did not feel different from them. He did not tower above them or close himself off.
"Sir, have you got a girl-friend?"
"No."
"Are you gay Sir?"
"No, but I do enjoy dressing up as a woman."
"Arhhh Sir!!"
"Only at the weekend mind."
"You don't."
"I like putting on a nice frock and walk through town on a Saturday and do a nice bit of shop-ping."
The children enjoyed the way that he joked with them and he earned respect for the entertain-ment value that he provided. His Year Seven class would fall apart laughing at the thought of him dressing like a woman at the weekend, his Year Eight likewise but more reserved and embarrassed, Year Ten began to look up to him and Year Eleven demanded to know who he screwed at the weekend.

Joseph found it funny; the kids found it funny, and on the whole the standard of work that he was receiving was very good and so he saw no harm in it at all. On the contrary, it was re-freshing for the children to witness first hand a world that did not patronise. The only problem was, was that Joseph did not really have a happy successful story to tell for the children to lis-ten to so he would use some invention. However the goal posts had moved, growth was in the air, the shape of the goal was altering or perhaps no-one was trying to score.

Chapter 10: Emma

Mrs Bylaw would send Emma off to school and disappear into the world of crime-busting in her crime-busting mobile quick on the heels of anyone who would dare to have the cheek to cross that line. She would go about her work with gusto, locking people up for fun to compensate for the way life had given her problems. It felt good to see other people suffering and it was a bonus to get paid for it. Don't ask why just lock them up. She would accuse, insist and coerce the unlucky and guilty because you don't get anywhere without a bit of force, do you? The unlucky would say the wrong thing and bang! Write it down, sign it, get it all down. Arhh, an inconsistency. Inconsistency means guilt. Send him down, down into a cold dark lonely cell.

Mrs Bylaw did not know that her daughter had found herself a special place in Joseph's heart. Emma Bylaw was a fiery character but she had the capacity to make Joseph laugh and Joseph hadn't got anyone who could do that. She wasn't the prettiest of girls but she was pretty and she fought her cause like a mother protecting her young. She would laugh, kick and scream, she would bring the house down if needs be to satisfy herself, her world and all those who lived freely in it. Joseph liked Emma because she expressed herself without reserve. She would honestly express her heart felt opinions and push the boundaries.

Emma saw through Joseph without knowing how far she saw; she touched his limit and pushed it. She was pushing it like a virgin giving birth. He did not know how the baby had got there but what he did know was that she had an effect on him. She would call him a doughnut when he displayed his ineptitude which made him try harder; she would be particularly nasty on occasions but he love her for it because it would inspire him to be a better man and it made him feel alive.

Emma was a Year Eleven pupil possessed by super powered hormones; she could be outra-geously difficult or funny depending on whether the moon had entered the orbit of Venus or Uranus. If the sun was shining and the birds were singing she would laugh and sing with all the good nature of the angels up above sitting on white fluffy clouds drumming their harp strings. If she felt shafted; teased; deceived; or led a merry dance, she would break into spon-taneous anger and unleash her wrath on all those around with the cold hearted determination of a brutal dictator.

Emma's teenage life was bound by rules and regulations; rules which did not cater for the hormonal curious young lady she was. Some needed these rules to give meaning and pur-pose to their life, others happened to fit in with the regulations, others found enjoyment in pushing them and discovering the life of a young adult which for most of them was their reality. Emma had individual needs just like the other members of the class but she would tend to push them to far greater extent than the others. For much of the time, the pushing was the pleasure rather than the end result.

She liked Joseph because he seemed to not know the rules in a kind of hapless manner. He would plough his own field whether it be wind, rain or snow. There he would be, back bent pulling that huge mechanical beast that cultivated the fertile land. He had clawed back his authority in the other classes but his Year Elevens were still somewhat adrift. Emma would sit at the back sucking her thumb wondering what his life was like and she demanded an answer from him.

Joseph's incipient feelings for Emma began to take hold of him. She could throw back his words and make him laugh. She could enrich them and burst into spontaneous laughter and in turn make him laugh. She seemed to be able to identify something ridiculous in what he was doing, uncovering it whereupon they would both laugh. The Year Elevens, however, had exams, important exams that may affect their future. Each lesson was determined by coursework or exam. The exams were coming up hard upon them:

"The unseen material is what distinguishes the Higher Tier paper from the Foundation Paper," said Joseph.

"How are we supposed to read and comment on something we can't see?" Asked Emma with deep amusement and sarcasm.

"You don't get to see the text before the exam but obviously it will be there for you to read once the exam commences," replied Joseph sighing.

"Now you will need to know the text from Other Cultures and it will be that you will be compar-ing the unseen text with. Now this text from another culture is obviously unusual. It is sup-posed to be unusual to us because it is not from our culture. Now we understand that the protagonist of the piece, that is the main character, has been cast out by his tribe. Why we don't know. You accept that he is all alone with no family or friends in the midst of the jungle. Now who can tell me what happens?" Said Joseph.

"He runs into a tribe of baboons Sir."

"Good. Then what?"

"The head baboon fights him and he kills the baboon dead."

"Good, and the what happens?"

"Sir, he's injured. He hides in the hollow of a tree to convalesce."

"Good, good word 'convalesce.' And in what way does the writer suggest the tree nurtures him?"

"He drinks the moisture that gathers in the well of the tree sir and he eats the bark."
"Good, and what is this likened to? What imagery is used to suggest a comparison with an-other state of life-giving, nurturing and growth?"
The room went silent as the girls pondered the impenetrable question. What could it be? No, no answer.
"What about the position of the man in the hollow of the tree?"
But still no answer. The man is curled up in the foetal position so the writer is making a direct link to a baby in a womb being nourished by its mother. Yes? "O" they said scratching their heads.
"So you will need to compare this piece with an extract which you don't get to see now but will see later. Okay Emma?"
"Yes, Sir," she said answering absent-mindedly and taking very little of what came before on board. She didn't want to listen, not to boring stuff.

The day of the Year Eleven pre-GCSE exam test arrived and Joseph descended the steps and sauntered into the concourse where the corridors met. He was looking over at the double doors that led to the hall. A sign had been put out which said, "Silence, Exam in Progress," and then Emma appeared before him. She wanted a reminder about what she was about to face:
"Sir, what's the piece that we have to do today about?" Asked Emma seizing on his presence and hoping to make last minute preparations.
"It's the text from another culture," said Joseph.
"Yeah, what's it about?"
"It's about this geezer who had a fight with a monkey," said Joseph reductively and employing a colloquial term.

Emma stared at him in bemusement. Half believing and half not believing the short reply which seemed to contravene the etiquette usually employed by the English department that would normally be expansive, artistic and conform to Standard English terminology. She was waiting for him to add to his descriptive account but noticing that he was done and increudulous at the prospect of putting his words down as an answer she said:
"Oh my God," with a smile of amusement and went off to join her friends and share the mo-ment. Joseph was left saying, "What? It is." Which it was but nevertheless.

It wasn't long before Christmas was upon them. They were all expected to watch a nativity play and thank God for sending his son. Joseph spent Christmas alone because his family were busy with their own activities and he had no friends. He was however contented and he had an enjoyable holiday. Joseph knew Emma affected him but he was so busy he did not stop to consider what might be happening to him. Furthermore, he was a teacher and she was a pupil and no relationship should happen between the two parties.

On their return from the Christmas break, Emma became more inquisitive; she had an interest in Joseph but she became stubborn and uncompromising when it was not reciprocated, when perhaps he was concentrating on work. Having got through their mock exams, he was now faced with the task of improving their coursework. Emma tended to be an awkward customer who did little work until perhaps the end when everything was hurried and deadlines had to be negotiated. She brought to Joseph a mixture of pleasure and pain. Whilst she could make him laugh, she could also hurt him. She could be disparaging about his teaching and yet they could share a joke. She could ask personal questions which he would find discomforting and yet flattering.

His feelings for Emma developed over time. She planted a seed in his heart which took time to grow; it steadily germinated and fronds sprouted this way and that. As the months passed shoots had developed into long twisting vines that reached down and up, up and down into his limbs until there was no place to go except the mind, that nebulous region where thoughts were tossed and turned, accepted, rejected, discarded and followed.

Across time, Emma showed little interest in Tennyson's tragic poem, The Lady of Shallot, nei-ther was she particularly enamoured by the activities of the calculating and manipulative Miss Jean Brodie. Similarly Richard the 3rd, sparked little interest. Her non-fiction piece consisted in an argument against the use of physical punishment in the rearing of children, her fictional piece was a tragic love story, involving a letter, which began with promise but rather petered out like much of her coursework.

The wintery weeks passed by and Emma sat back and took it easy. Snowmen were made and melted; half term came and went and still no coursework was handed in. The deadline was looming large; she had the intelligence to do it (to do very well) but she just would not do it. And then, just before the deadline arrived, pieces of work were submitted. Predictively, however, Emma failed to get a piece in by the deadline but Joseph bent the rules for her and one or two others. It was with dismay therefore that he greeted her misbehaviour after he had just stuck his neck out for her:

"Emma, will you be quiet," for she was talking quite openly whilst he was trying to convey a message. "Emma, stop talking."
"Right outside. Your staying in during break-time also." She looked at him with disgust. And perhaps now they had adopted the real teacher-pupil relationship with her on one-side and him on the other. But she was wondering what she had done wrong? What gave him the right to determine that she should stay back? She starred at him angrily. She did not like anyone who stopped her getting her own way. She held a grudge and determined that Joseph would pay for his behaviour towards her.

It bugged her all day. She went home feeling like a victim cruelly attacked by a nasty man. She stored-up her anger deep inside and waited for the following lesson. She spoke out of turn, she referred to other boys hoping to arouse his jealousy, the lesson passed but she had not seen a reaction. Did he care? She sat at home thinking about him. She ate an Easter egg for comfort and resolved on retribution. She grew madder and doubled her efforts. The next day, she ascended the stairs to higher places with the resolve to make him suffer this lesson and in clear voluminous speech she told him:
"I don't like you…"
"Stop looking at me," she spoke in defiance and in a way determined to end their relationship.
She had landed a blow so deep that Joseph felt his being derail for he must by now love her. He ignored her but she had hurt him. She and the rest of the class left him like a wounded soldier slumped in his chair adrift of the desk He walked around the school hurt; moisture gave his eyes a glazed look which made him resemble at times, Heather Firk. Emma had got what she wanted.

Emma had landed the blow, she knew it, and the next lesson seemed to be about reparations for she sat closer to the front, behaved and contributed to the lesson thus restoring the bond which was now perhaps stronger for their bust-up which had seen them each test each other's sensibilities. She had backed down and resolved the feud and he had accepted her terms. Their relationship was by no means perfect but there were moments of mutual tenderness.

She was interested in his business and he liked the attention she gave him. She wanted to know why he wasn't at the Year Eleven party, she wanted to know what his flat was like, she wanted to arrange a party, she wanted to know why he didn't have a better car. She wanted to know if he had a girl-friend yet, what pet names he had for her, how many girls he had been out with and such like questions. She was dissatisfied with certain answers and concluded that he must be gay; but he did not seem gay.

She was getting stroppier and more temperamental as the days got longer and warmer. She was finding the system more and more confining and her moods got more intense and as Jo-seph was moving around the classroom and passed her chair she said half audibly, half muf-fled:
"I love you." And she looked half up at Joseph with defiance.
"Sorry," said Joseph with emphasis like a question for he had heard but not understood properly in that moment.
Her face contorted as she interpreted his reply as a rejection. She was just a school kid; she was not going to have any success with him. She swallowed the painful truth and promptly demanded permission to visit the toilet. She put the lid down on the toilet and sat there in pri-vate misery. She got up, went to the

sink and washed her face and braced herself. She looked in the mirror and felt whole and cleared away any signs of distress and took herself back up to the classroom where she set about her work.

Her birthday was coming up fast upon her. Joseph had found her difficult but manageable if she felt she was being catered for. She wanted a present and he knew that she would be childlike without some token of affection and secretly he wanted to get her something. He de-cided to buy her a dummy. Something to sick in her when she moans, groans and needs pla-cating. It was there to replace her thumb which she enjoyed sucking. It would be something to bring relief when everything bestial wells up inside.

She would like that; it would bring pain and pleasure to Emma's sensibility. Pain for suggest-ing that she's an immature big baby and pleasure for he had thought of her and delivered. She came into the classroom hot and bothered. Hard work that was the order of the day. How long did she have to endure this sentence? Her legs twitched remorselessly, Joseph droned on and on and on about the literary merits of a piece from the pre-release material, she had had enough. She collapsed half exhausted, half ready for sport:
"Did you have a nice birthday?" asked Joseph.
"Yes, can I go to the toilet?" Asked Emma.
"Did you get Emma a birthday present?" Intervened Sarah.
"Yeah, where's my birthday present?" demanded Emma.
"You can have it at the end of the lesson."
"You got me one?"
"I might have done."
"Well, where is it."
"I haven't got it on me."

"arhh well you can forget it," she said with annoyance and displeasure.
"No, I've got it but it isn't to hand. It's in the classroom but you can only have it at the end of the lesson.
"Can I go to the toilet?" She asked cheering-up.
Emma left the classroom full of wonder. Had he thought of her? Had he actually gone out and bought something special for her birthday? But now she was slightly afraid. What could it be? Had she won his affection? Did she want it after all? As she approached the toilets she felt she was stepping out into unchartered territory.

The toilets were the same. They were the ones she had frequently used. She had sat on that toilet on many occasions. She dropped her knickers and rested her thighs on the white seat ring. She wiped herself clean and pulled up her knickers with calm assurance. She had de-posited many depository sanitary towels in the special deposal unit. Now, as she looked at herself in the minor, her reflection looked back at her with stern eyes.

She splashed water across her face. She needed to wake herself-up. She collected her thoughts and gathered herself-up, braced herself and took herself off back up the stairs to the classroom, sat in her seat and crossed her legs. She wondered what he could have for her. As time passed she grew increasingly nervous. The bell would sound any moment now. It would be her time. She and she alone would have to face the bell ringing, ringing for all its might. What would it bring? The horror of change or the ecstasy of new horizons? She had set the ball in motion; she had asked for this but did she want it? How could she know when she had never set sail for this particular destination? The lighthouse standing proud would guarantee her safety surely?

She jumped as the bell sounded. The other girls were packing their things away and taking themselves off to their timetabled next period like they had done before. But Emma had opened up something new and she suddenly felt vulnerable. She gripped her legs together and stood up. Things needed to go in her bag; she collected herself. She stood in amongst her circle of friends and edged over to Joseph sitting at his desk at the front and in the centre of the classroom. At the same time she edged towards the classroom door at the front but to-ward the side of the classroom. She seemed to be drawn towards both. Was she going to be split in two?

Joseph looked up at her. She looked in his direction but she was scared.
"You get it for me," said Emma to Sarah.
Sarah did not reply but she did not approach Joseph for he had not asked her to take the gift and pass it on; she was half in a mind to give in but he would have to ask her to take it for Emma. Seeing that Emma was hesitant, Joseph retorted; "Well, if you don't want it." Where-upon Emma made tiny little nervous steps towards him; she stopped just short of his desk; close enough to accept a gift but not so close that she could be swept off her feet and be dragged deep down into the underworld. Her legs twitched. Joseph lifted his hand and place it on the handle of his desk draw. He eased it open and then it slammed shut with a force greater than Joseph had been aware of.

He held her gift in a transparent bag. He held it up to her not touching what lay inside.
"This is for you when you get angry and things aren't going your way. You can take this and it will relax you," said Joseph with a steady voice but an unsure mind.

She took the bag from him and placed her hand inside. She took out the pink dummy that lay inside. It was perched on the tip of her thumb and index finger. She was delighted, she was flabbergasted. She did not know what to think. He had given her something to fill a hole, the transparent bag was left flapping in the wind; she loved it, she hated it; was he calling her a baby or was he treating her like a grown-up?

Her friends looked at it. They touched it, passed it around.
"Do you want it?" said Sarah having gazed at it with a mixture of delight and jealousy. Emma looked at her and took it with a grin on her face. She came down on the side of pleasure. She did not know what it said, she was not entirely happy with it but she wanted it all the same. And so she took it before her friend did and left with a feeling of triumph. She departed the classroom and descended the stairs.

The last day of the school year, the last day before study leave was clearly in sight for Emma and the rest of Year Eleven. Nobody was doing work on the last day. It was an emotional day when the pupils were given the opportunity to say goodbye to their time in compulsory educa-tion and all that that had entailed. Emma stepped into the English classroom for the last time. She sat on a seat by Joseph's desk:
"How will you remember me?" she asked with interest.
"As a big character," replied Joseph not fully admitting to the feelings he had acquired for her. They chatted freely and listened to music. The bell sounded and announced the end of their relationship. Joseph felt crestfallen as she left:
"Bye Sir," she said, and her face contorted and she broke into tears.
Joseph smiled wistfully, feeling every bit as upset.

Mrs Bylaw collected Emma at the school gates dead on sixteen hundred hours although she stood there before defiant refusing to acknowledge the onward motion of time. Emma jumped into the crime busting mobile while her dummy lay concealed within and Mrs Bylaw drove off home feeling quite satisfied because she had not long since locked up a trouble maker.

Chapter 11: Study Skills

The old oak tree was being robbed of its clothing. It stood grinning and bearing the shortening days and the long cold nights. Squirrels had raced up its trunk and across its branches. The wind had taken its fruit and leaves. A woodpecker had sought relief in a whole in its front. It flew in and out as it pleased, and the school children went past twice daily whilst it remained rooted to the spot.

She wasn't particularly noticeable. She rarely started trouble but trouble seemed to follow her around like a dirty hand to a pair of lacy knickers. She existed behind a glassy exterior; gazing out through tears whilst life continued around her unconcerned and not wishing to be concerned. Her friends laughed gaily in the playground, the teachers had their registers to call and Mrs Bylaw whizzed past in her crime busting mobile. So she stayed behind that glassy exterior.

She had little respect for appearances; my appearance, your appearance and least of all her own appearance. It what's inside that's important she thought. She did not like to wear school uniform like all the other children. She liked to hang her shirt out, loosen her tie and undo a button here, a button there. She would wear an over-grown crucifix around her neck as if to make her prayers more voluminous and she would lavish copious amounts of make-up on her face as if to create another face.

She had little time for polite conversation. Her language was often explicit and her actions showed a flagrant disregard of the rules. The trouble that followed her around jumped on her and seized her. It penetrated her being and oozed inside every available orifice. It spread in-side of her until she was so caught up in the trouble that she no longer knew that trouble was giving her the reputation of not just being trouble but being a trouble-maker. She had made no trouble; it had crept after her. She had been cornered in a dark room when all of a sudden Cyclops spat at her. She did not make trouble, how could she of all people make trouble? She was not a trouble-maker but a trouble-taker. And so she would, as she gazed out of her glassy world, think of England and its pleasant green lands.

She turned up to school each day. She liked to get out of the house and breathe the fresh air. She would feel empathy as she walked past the old oak tree that stuck to the ground as fury animals crept around it. She was in day in day out; her appearance was dishevelled and heavy with lipstick but that aside she looked on the surface like the other school children. She belonged to the community that was the school even if she was a little different. Her name was known in the school community for it was synonymous with trouble and maker. The teachers said her name with disapproval and many children eyed her with a mixture of fear and awe for she, as was commonly agreed by the teachers, was a bad one.

Joseph met Heather Firk once a week for Study Skills. Study Skills presented its own prob-lems. It wasn't Joseph's trained subject, there was no National Curriculum to follow, there was no exam paper with right and wrong and a marking scheme to follow that defined terms under which a judgement of success could be made. No, it was imposed on him and the children and they had to deal with it the best way possible. Many of the pupils saw it as a "doss" subject.

The years work for Study Skills consisted of three projects; one for the autumn, winter and spring term.

The subject was taken in middle school above Ms Proper's teaching room in the computer suite. Each student had a computer to develop their information technology skills. On the computer were the different Microsoft applications, the internet, e-mail and a facility to listen to music. As the work was not curriculum led and results orientated, Joseph saw no harm in allowing the pupils listen to music as they worked.

In the turbulent, blustery autumn term they were to start a relationship. It had to be straight; there's no way we can have homosexuality openly discussed in the classroom of a Roman Catholic School. Mrs Standard would consume faggots in the school canteen and that's fine; as long as it's meat taken inside the mouth, taken in and swallowed, that's fine, but do not, do not speak about a homosexual relationship within the Catholic School:
"Now class, what you are being asked to do is to imagine that you don't get out much. You're a bit sad and you decide to join a dating agency in the hope of meeting your true love. What you need to do is plot the relationship from the first email to phone call, the first date, second, dinner perhaps all the way through to engagement and marriage."
Predictably, Heather's Lonely Hearts project was rather explicit but it was something that she could do and she generally enjoyed pretending to be somebody else looking for someone who might love that someone who wasn't her. She enjoyed charting the development of a man robbing a girl of her innocence. She sat on her red cushioned swivel chair and lent back against the purple garment slung carelessly over it and delineated his each and every move.

The old oak tree now stood completely bear and bereft of any cover. The cold dark winter term project consisted in an exchange:

"Now class, what you are being asked to do is to pretend that you are host to a foreign ex-change student. You need to write a guide book and planner to help the student to cope in this country and to give him or her an itinery of things to do."
"I don't want an exchange student sir. Can't they just stay in France?"
"No, they are coming to your house and its your responsibility to look after them."
"But the French are greasy and they smell."
Two-thirds of the pupils provided guides which would help foreign visitors whilst the rest pro-duced guides that would confound, confuse and discombobulate their guests. Of course there were different extremes; pupils with responsible and caring parents would tend to extend that care to their visitors. They would expect their guests to abide by the house rules but in return they would get warmth and security; a room of their own with a lock and key. They would be given reliable information, correct numbers, a mobile phone with calling credit should they find themselves in trouble and need saving.

Then there were those who would tease; the number for the local police station would turn out to be the number for the local pizzeria but thankfully the number for the fast-food takeaway would turn out to be the coppers. The guests of these children would get a mobile but only a small amount of calling credit so it was incumbent upon the visitor to use the calling credit wisely or it would be gone and then what are you going to do?

Then there were those who did not know how to play the humble host. In these households doors were locked. People were locked inside whilst the outside world did not venture to con-cern itself with this crime often committed within family relations. Each box was seen to con-tain a happy family but was this the truth? What meanness was being committed within the households where power relations were unleashed? What one did in the privacy of the family home was confidential so fuck off said the father playing, the mother browsing the catalogue and the bomber devising.

The guests of these people were given a mobile with infinite calling credit but the speaker and receiver was the wrong way round. Nobody was listening and you could not speak anyway because the mouth piece contained a deep sound that thrust itself into your open mouth. The numbers were jumbled, who was there to call? Leave a message and hope…

The spring term saw the return of more clement weather and the harshness of winter retreat into the background. The old oak tree began to cloth itself in green and restore its dignity, green shrubs could be seen sprouting up around the school and the water-logged field was beginning to dry. The children were drawn by the sun and soon they would be let loose on the grassy pasture to release unspent energy.

The project for this term was to write a story to a specific audience. Joseph was a blank piece of paper upon which they could write their stories. They could write for either young children or they could write a story for their peers (youngish teenagers). Those who opted for the young children's story produced a simpler story that involved repetition with incremental changes illustrated by pictures. Those who chose to write for teenagers had licence to write about more complex ideas but they were constrained by the bounds of decency.

Their stories were active stories; imaginative stories which spoke of innocent adventure. There were friendship, love, hatred and betrayal and then there wasn't a story, a story that did not speak at all. It did not speak because of the nature of the story and its implications. It was a story that could not be accepted by society.

Heather decided to write a story aimed at younger children. She could not however take the project seriously. Farmer Joseph, she decided upon, the enforcer of particular stories, would go and feed the animals down the farm. He would feed the pigs, the cows, the chickens... but she lost impetuous and rejected the direction of the story or what it could mean. Her story lacked punch and it tailed off after half a page because she could not believe in her story and she felt betrayed and patronised by it.
"I don't like writing stories," complained Heather.
"Well why don't you try writing the other type of story," suggested Joseph.
"I don't want to," she replied.
"Come on. Try writing a story about teenagers and what it is like to be a teenager in the 21st Century," said Joseph encouragingly.
"I can't because we are not allowed to write about swearing, drugs and sex," said Heather.
Heather remained convinced that story telling was impossible for her. It was a task that she was unable to engage with and so Joseph set about thinking of an alternative project she could undertake. He was not going to have this trouble-taker making trouble in his lesson. No, he needed to find an alternative.

The music lifted and fell; it glided and it dipped. The children were plugged into their own little world listening to each of the different tracks with varying degrees of enjoyment. Some were listening to certain

CDs because they were cool, some because they enjoyed the sounds and some because they actually identified with the lyrics. There was rap, R&B, speed garage, house, pop and rock. Horses for courses as they say. For some the outside world became irrelevant as they became subsumed by the rhythm, they tapped idly as they delved into the darker reaches of their stories.

Heather became animated by the lyrics of the rap artists. "Fuck the bitch, the bitch has been born for fucking. Show me a bitch who don't like dick … etc." "Listen to that…listen.. listen," she would exclaim excitedly. "Did you hear that? Did you?" Joseph noticed the way that Heather found something in the lyrics that excited her and this gave him an idea. He noticed the way that the red cushioned swivel chair with the purple garment slung over the back seemed to bring her alive when this music was playing. It pushed her up and down, she could not sit still, in and out of her chair petitioning and interfering with her classmates as they worked; if Heather could not write a story maybe she could do work based on the songs that she liked listening to. Maybe Joseph could channel this energy productively.

Noticing Heather's affinity to the rap music of her generation, Joseph thought to himself that this might be a window into her life. A glimpse of what is going on behind the doors of that particular household. If he could just look in, then maybe, just maybe, he could find a place, a place for her within the school where she could express herself and get credit for what she produced instead of the constant criticism that seemed to follow her around.

The idea occurred to Joseph overnight. One morning he emerged out of the staffroom. He saw Heather sat

on a bench in the concourse where the corridors met and where the stairs led to higher places waiting to be climbed. As usual she looked up but remained mute when confronted by a teacher. She could not speak out.
"Hello Heather," said Joseph.
"Hi Sir," replied Heather.
"I was thinking, could you make a list of your favourite artists and songs for me?" asked Joseph hopefully.
"Yeah okay. I saw you last night at Sainsbury's" said Heather.
"Oh, I must have missed you. Doing some shopping were you?" said Joseph.
"My mum was. We live just round the corner," revealed Heather.
"Handy for home then?" continued Joseph.
"Yes, is it for you?" wondered Heather.
"Its fairly close, I live in a little flat on the top floor in Hope Village," said Joseph absent-mindedly.
"Why do you want a list of songs?" Inquired Heather with interest.
"I was thinking that if you can't write a story you could do some work around music," said Jo-seph disappearing into the distance as he did not want to arouse any suspicion. It was as if a cul-de-sac had been transformed into an avenue. She disappeared with her friend eagerly set on producing a list.

The next Study Skills lesson arrived but Joseph was dismayed to find that Heather had not done a list. She had compiled a number of songs but they had been drowned out and myste-riously lost amongst muffled voices.
"Okay," said Joseph, "do another one."
Heather set about writing another one but there seemed to be reluctance on her part.

"What do you want one for?" she asked suspiciously but at the same time pleased that some-one was poking their nose in.

She did not want to produce a list that revealed too much. "What's the name of that song by 50 cent?" she asked her friend. She did not create the list with the confidence of someone doing a task for the second time. Joseph was concerned that the list she did present to him was watered down. That it did not contain the songs that she really identified with but songs of more of a passing interest.
"You're not giving me the songs you really identify with," protested Joseph.
"Well, I can't," complained Heather.
"Why not," inquired Joseph.
"Because there are swear words in the lyrics," replied Heather with a bashfulness that did not usually belong to her.
Heather would swear with wild abandonment when she knew that it was prohibited. Joseph seemed to be giving her the chance to present material of an explicit nature but now it dis-turbed her. She grew strangely coy. Joseph thought her excuse about prohibited language was a smoke-screen. If she did not care about swearing to a teacher why would she be con-cerned about giving the name of a song containing explicit lyrics? It was not as if she had to utter the words. The door was creaking shut, soon it would slam in his face and the lock would turn.

Joseph managed to cajole Heather into producing a list but he could not contain his annoy-ance at her apparent reluctance to speak out truthfully. His frustration boiled over into anger. He shouted at her, she was dismayed, she sat down on her swivel chair with its red cushion and purple garment slung over, and span. She stared at her screen. <HELP AND

SUPPORT> <SEARCH> <IRK> <0 RESULTS FOUND> <ENTER NEW SEARCH>. Joseph saw "Whiskey Bar," by the Doors crossed out.

Chapter 12: Maturity

The days were beginning to compete more favourably with the nights. The mornings were warmer and the worst of the coldness was over. Shoots were beginning to appear on the trees and clothes for the spring season were beginning to appear in the shops and on consumers. The weeks passed and Joseph was performing well. In the third term Joseph was ready for Mrs Standards appraisal.

Mrs standard patrolled the corridors. She stood in the doorway of the central concourse ad-ministering dictates, admonishing exuberance and stamping down the law across the school.
"Now we need to set a date for a lesson observation Joseph. Having missed an observation from the second term it's imperative that we get another under our belts," said Mrs standard
"Okay," said Joseph, "How about the Year Tens. Period one on Thursday," continued Joseph.
"Okay, Thursday it is," said Mrs standard.
With that settled Joseph picked himself up and left Mrs standard's rather comfortable office stationed adjacent to the toilets. He stepped outside through the central concourse where the corridors converged across the opening and up the stairs.

Joseph was improving, the timetable was beginning to ease with the year 11 pupils having gone on study leave and whilst there was much to do and there was no let-up in the intensity of pressure to succeed, Joseph was able to dedicate more time to lesson preparation and the individual needs of pupils in each of his remaining classes.

Joseph was beginning to assert himself for the first time. He was beginning to lead from the front whilst desisting from tyranny. He would go to much length to explain why he was doing what he was doing, he would be at pains to explain why so and so's behaviour was unac-ceptable and slowly but surely he was beginning to win over the pupils without having rejected any.

On the contrary, any exclusion occurred on the part of a select group of high fly fliers. A few girls and the odd boy had noticed his indecision, his accent and his disdain for etiquette and had decided that they could lead. He had whittled this group down until he had dragged each pupil back into the fold. He had a force on his side that cajoled the most awkward character to drop their hostility and accept his approach, for he was now really beginning to produce some quality lessons where once he stuttered now he purred.

The Year Ten's drooled over Leonardo Di Caprio playing Romeo, Joseph eased them into compliant pupils consuming stimulating material. The movie provided a back-drop for the play. It gave a semi-accurate portrayal of the story-line and a mental image of the characters involved which provided a base to teach from. It was a good introduction to the play but it sometimes failed to convey the sinister sexual energy and immediacy of events that unfolded.

The reading of the play was a laborious act. The language was in many places, for the pupils, impenetrable. Their innocence stood in direct opposition to Shakespeare's worldliness; it was Joseph's job to bridge the two. It was a difficult task to succeed at. There were twenty-seven different pupils all with differing levels of knowledge, interest and capability. Where one needed help another needed stimulating, where one was fascinated another gazed longingly through the window at the boys on the sports field and where one understood another remained unaware.

Joseph helped the pupils as best he could. He interrupted the reading from time to time to re-cap on events; he explained innuendo and he drew attention of the girls looking through the window, that transparent division, back and forth, back and forth until no division seemed to exist, only a game which they were learning about and thinking of playing in. Finally they reached the end. A sigh and a cheer emanated from those who were still concentrating on the text and those who were just aware that the ordeal was over. The pupils had now been given a good taste of the beauty and cheek of Shakespeare.

Joseph's teaching wasn't perfect by any means but having reached the third term, and having made his way half way through this last remaining term before the end of the year, he had improved considerably. He knew that he had something to offer the profession and he knew he had developed a rapport with the pupils that few other teachers could match.

He was accumulating schemes of work, he was learning how to mark accurately according to the marking scheme, he was marking homework much more quickly and he was acquiring presence in front of the class. He still had six weeks before the summer holidays; he needed to keep it up; he still wondered what to do with the kids tomorrow. What would the kids find interesting and different from before? He was beginning to rise up and sit comfortably on top of it all.

He still had lessons that were disorganised but once these last weeks had been conquered, he would have the security of having done it all before to take into the following year. He would be able to take that into the new term of the year and deliver it with confidence and verve. No more worry about what to do next, no more anxiety about the unknown and all that it can unexpectedly throw at you, no more worry about being outdone by the other pupils.

The Year Tens had been guided through Romeo and Juliet with assurance and insight. The culmination of their efforts was to be observed and judged by Mrs Standard. The Year Tens had deferred to Joseph; he had a hold over them which he had earned through hard work. As his lessons improved over the year they trusted his judgement and they felt a degree of security under his tutelage.

Joseph was aware that they did not want to see him fail. He had been shaky at the start, they could have turned on him, but generally they were on his side because he taught with a smile on his face and a willingness to listen.
Their affinity towards him grew each day. It was on this basis therefore that he decided to tell them that Mrs Standard was coming to judge him not them; that it was he who had to pass certain obstacles to progress in his career:
"On Thursday class, Mrs Standard is coming in to watch our lesson. She is coming in to watch me to make sure I am teaching you properly," confessed Joseph.
"Why? You are Sir," said Sophie.
"It's just because I am new," answered Joseph, "so I will have to do everything properly; call the register at the beginning and be quite formal. I will be expecting you to be on your best behaviour too. The only thing is, Mrs Standard might say she has come in to see you, but she is just taking the pressure off me."
"She's lying," said Sophie distrustfully.

"No, she is just helping out an inexperienced teacher," said Joseph.
"Sophie starred back at him unconvinced.

Mrs Standard was sat on a stool staring at the computer screen in the staffroom when Joseph entered. She was completing some necessary administration and Joseph was putting the kettle on.
"I've told the Year Ten that you are coming into the lesson tomorrow morning," he informed her. "They know that you're coming in to judge me rather than them."
"Okay, you're taking on the responsibility; you're taking it full on the chin like a man are you?" asked Mrs Standard rhetorically.
"I thought I would let you know just in case you said at the end that you had come into see them, like you sometimes do. I didn't want to put you in an awkward position," replied Joseph. At this Mrs Standard's face buckled. It was only momentary but a definite twist contorted her face. She recovered, repressed the spasm and sent it back, deep down where no one would see it again.
"Right, so I'll just say thanks for seeing the lesson and that will be enough," said Mrs Standard adjusting painfully to Joseph's way. "We'll see how you cope, now I must get on," continued Mrs Standard recoiling dismissedly. And so Joseph stirred his tea, pulled out the spoon, left the staffroom and ascended the stairs to a higher place.

She sat sternly at the back of the room with her pen at the ready to put down anything that came up short. Unbeknown to her the children were lined up outside in single file, perfectly obedient. Some of the leaders of the class had seen to that. Joseph ascended the stairs and found them ready to do him proud.

"Jesus," said Joseph, not surprised in theory to see them thus but unaccustomed to the reality. The children beamed back in embarrassed pleasure.
"In you go then," said Joseph.
And in they went, single file, like a troop of regimented soldiers marching to meet their fate be-cause someone had blundered but who? They sat down each in their place patiently awaiting guidance and instruction: "Jessica, Sir, Charlotte Sir, Stacy Sir… "Right, you don't need your exercise books this morn-ing, just your pens and pencils," said Joseph. "Today we're going to do a number of exercises on Romeo & Juliet which are designed to improve your knowledge of the play. Now, we all know that this play is a tragic love story but you are probably less aware about the rapidity of the play. You do not experience the speed at which events unfold in the film, its rather mis-leading. In actual fact, this play starts on Sunday, God's day of rest, and finishes within a week, on Thursday I think, not even a week. Now, can anyone tell me why Shakespeare packs all the action into a small amount of time?"
"Because it's a play about passion and following your heart rather than law and tradition. If it took a long time there would be a feeling of design, planning and sobriety but Shakespeare wants to portray impassioned star crossed lovers," said Sophie.
"Good, it's a play about following your heart without reserve. Now, have a look at the work-sheet, on the grid you have a list of different events that occur in the play. Now it's your job to put the correct day, and the time of day with the event."
The pupils settled to the task at hand. They each worked diligently and there was much chat-ter to be heard concerning the play.
"Can you put your pens down and listen a moment whether you have finished or not please? Right, when you have finished I would like you to consider the concept of responsibility. Who is responsible for the

tragic events that unfold? Can you make a list of the characters and the creator and state why you consider that they, he or she, might be said to be responsible.

And so they each decided who was to blame. Mrs Standard sat judging and the kids judged the characters and Joseph knew he had put on a lesson that purred. Mrs Standard thanked them for their time and said what pleasure it was to see them at work and off she went down the stairs in pursuit of her comfortable office by the staff toilets.

Chapter 13: Exuberance and Signs of Mania

Joseph was starting to get off on the success that he was deriving from the classroom. His mind was going in different directions, he was forever thinking about the kids and the work and he was putting in long hours. He was drinking in the evening to calm down and he was waking early and starting work before going to school.

Joseph had probably been drinking too much ever since his second year of university but now he was really getting a taste for it. He would look forward to it as the bell for the end of school time approached. He would leave as soon as possible and get in his car and speed home. He would get through the front door, drop his bags and open a bottle of larger.

He would have all sorts of thoughts about the school day and the beer would settle his mind. It would help him to think about the day more accurately and then, when he had had maybe three of four, he would start to think about what to do about any problem that had arisen at school. The beer would calm him, give him ideas and then arm him with the confidence to do what he needed to do about it.

Year Ten parent's evening finished and Joseph got in his car, sped off home and opened a bottle of larger. He reflected upon the evening: all the parents were satisfied with what he had said except perhaps for Cindy's parents for she was not getting the grades. Her language use was at times awkward and it felt forced as if someone was putting her under pressure. Her father wanted to know what she was doing wrong and so, Joseph took out a sample of her work and displayed the problem for them to see.

In order to help Cindy, Joseph agreed to help her during lunch-time. Mandy's mother was surprised to hear from Joseph that she had a good speaking voice and that she was doing well in her oral assessment for she wore braces said her mother and would often cover her mouth when talking so other people could not see them. Joseph had not thought of a response at the time, but as he supped his beer he thought that his class was an all girl's class and in such an environment she would feel less embarrassed.

Joseph began to think about tomorrow. There was a rotund ginger girl in his year seven form tutor class who also worried about her appearance. She would complain that she was fat and nobody would like her. Her mother had been in trouble a number of times because she had been violent and she had learnt how to hit out too. Frequently would Joseph see her lashing out at her neighbour: Joseph was exasperated. He was sick of her complaining and hitting other children and the next day he took her aside and told her that there was nothing wrong with her, that it did not matter if she was over-weight, she could still have a happy and fulfilling life but she had to stop complaining and hitting out at people and start valuing what she did have. Joseph praised her singing for she could sing very well and he reminded her that the boy, Willie, who sat next to her in form class and who also was not small, might be interested in her for they got on very well when she was not punching him.

The words seemed to have an effect on her. They seemed to undermine what she had thought to be true. Was Willie interested in her? As Joseph sent her off to assembly for it was still early in the morning, she forgot to leave her bag in the form room and went off to the hall with it on her back unaware of its presence as she was consumed by new thoughts. Joseph got a buzz from solving their problems and opening doors for them and it gave him a feeling of being special. Not only did he feel whole now, as if his two selves had come together, he felt privileged as he was helping others. He found himself talking to himself when he was alone; he would anticipate conversations and situations and would plan out what he was going to say and what might make people laugh.

Whilst he did not have a girl-friend or any other private life to speak of, he was beginning to feel that he was part of a community and he was an important member of that community. He felt whole, he felt excited by the future but he also felt a need to take risks; to gamble with what he had earned. As he walked from middle school to lower school he cut across the grass; this was forbidden as children would come into classrooms with muddy feet, only the designated playing fields on fine days were permitted. As Joseph ventured into forbidden territory he scolded a couple of his year elevens who were passing walking on the path for walking on the grass to which they laughed.

One morning he came into work and informed his year ten girls that there are certain things you need to do by the time your thirty and one of those is to sleep with someone old enough to be your mother, on another he came in with no tie on and when he looked up his year ten class had all loosened or taken their ties off too. Another morning, after a nights drinking, he was escorting his year sevens to assembly whereupon they had lost him and gone to the other of the two doors that led to the hall only to find the door locked. Joseph had gone in through the open door and sat with the other teachers.
"Joseph, where's your class?" asked the Head of House.

Joseph looked up; they should be sat at the front where the year sevens always sit but they were nowhere to be seen. A puzzled expression appeared on Joseph's face and he scratched his chin. Emma had been watching him and as he went to look for his lost class, she shouted out, "Sir," to which Joseph replied with a smirk, "I've lost my class."

The next time Joseph was to see Emma was in a Resistant Materials exam. As he drank larg-er of an evening he would think about what to do in class, what would help and amuse his classes and he thought how nice it would be if he could be with Emma. He did not know she would be sitting in the woodwork exam and he would be invigilating but fate had brought them together. She sat perched on her stool looking beautiful.
"I bought a disco dick yesterday," she said to Joseph.
"What's that?" Inquired Joseph.
"A vibrator," replied Emma.
"Ooh," said Joseph, "Can't you find anyone to do it for you?" he asked unkindly.
"Don't be horrible to me," she said. "He's done it," she said motioning towards one of her peers. Joseph saw the competition and was then asked to hand out the exam papers. The Year Elevens were now to sit in silence.

Joseph observed at a distance. Occasionally he would look at Emma and think "should I?" He took out a piece of paper and wrote, "I love you." He tore around the words and folded-up the piece of paper. He wanted to take the risk, he was driven towards it but he needed an excuse: an excuse to walk past Emma and slip it onto her desk. He felt rooted to the spot like the old oak tree without an excuse because he couldn't reveal his true motive.

It was coming towards the end of the period he was designated for invigilation and another teacher would soon appear to take over. Joseph thought he would never tell her and she would leave his life ignorant. As he looked at her, she looked up and looked at him and mouthed the words, "fuck off," in a warm hearted way. Joseph smiled back and walked to-wards her desk. He walked around to where Emma was perched with the screwed-up piece of paper in his fingers. Emma lifted her arms and directed her pen as if ready to start work again. Joseph came in beside her put the little piece of paper on her desk and flicked it forward. He then retreated whereupon she grabbed the love note. He did not want to see her and she was absorbing the information.

When the other teacher appeared, Joseph was free to go to his next period. He glanced at Emma as he left the room and she looked at him with an expression of distrust. Joseph had crossed a line and she didn't like it.

Chapter 14: Irk

It was a tempestuous evening; the skies were angry, God had gone missing and in his ab-sence the animal kingdom fought itself into an orgy of senselessness. The school bell signalling home-time had long since rung, darkness had descended and it would not be long now till the children were to go to bed. The skies cracked with pain, spears of lightning fury plunged down deeply and the rain hammered the floor. God's little creatures had scurried into any available orifice hoping to find safety in the middle of the pouring rain. The door blew open and shut but who had the keys?

At that moment a bow could be heard crashing to the ground. Lightning had struck the old oak tree which refused to stand silently by any longer. Like a self-harmer; it creaked, "take my limb; take it as recompense for a life short lived, cut short by the cruel hand of fate," and down it crashed to the ground.

Mr Firk had arrived home from work at the slaughter house. He had brought home a joint of meat slaughtered at his own hand. He had grabbed the beast from around the neck and looked full into its glassy eyes as he ripped a blade across its throat. There was no rhyme nor reason, ethics or good will, just taste, self-interest and survival of the fittest and he prided him-self on the fact that he faced the truth. He did not get anyone else to do his dirty-work. He did not go into the convenience store and buy a deceitfully prepared meat which divorced the act of butchery from that of consumption and dinner table silver etiquette. No, it was far more honest, he saw life and he usually over-powered people because they did not look.

He unlocked the door and took bold strides into his house. He placed the meat down on the side in the kitchen ready for his wife to prepare. He opened the fridge and took out a can of larger; with that in hand he went into the living room and dropped into a chair. He pulled the ring pull and took a sip and wiped the froth from his facial hair:

"Get that roast on, I'm starving," shouted Mr Firk to Mrs Firk who had just descended the stairs.

"Okay, it will be a couple of hours,"she replied bitterly as she had spent all day in Iceland serv-ing at the check out and she was tired.

"Make sure it's only a couple," said Mr Firk.

Mrs Firk set about preparing dinner. She put the meat in the oven; she took out some potatoes and then set about preparing the vegetables. It was not long before the kitchen was hot with steam and the pungent smell of meat roasting. Each hob was firing away and pots bubbled with sprouts bobbing to the top now and then showing their green wrapped leaves.

"Kids, dinner will be ready in ten minutes," she bellowed up the stairs.

Timing was of the essence of producing a good hot meal. Each thing ought to be cooked to its time and they should each finish together despite taking different times for completion. Mrs Firk found the end the most distressing part of cooking. Could she bring it off together? Seldom ever do things fall all together. She would get angry and shout at the children as if they were to blame for her inability to balance the different components and she would demand that they ate all their vegetables which she knew they did not particularly like.

Ten minutes turned into fifteen which turned into twenty which turned into thirty and then, fourty-five. Mrs Firk was furious, Mr Firk was fuming and the kids were flabbergasted for they had been made to wait at the table for the best part of half an hour until freshly cut meat ar-rived on the centre of the table. There were also potatoes, carrots, peas, runner beans and sprouts.

Mummy and daddy took lots of meat, potatoes and vegetables, Julie, Heather and Nicky each in their turn took plenty of meat, some potatoes and a few vegetables.
"Take some vegetables," said Mrs Firk in a tone that left no room for compromise.
"I got enough," said Julie.
"You haven't got enough," replied Mrs Firk.
Each child put some vegetables on their plate to satisfy Mrs Firk but they did not intend to eat them. There was little conversation as each family member tucked in."Your not leaving the table until you have eaten all your vegetables," said Mrs Firk."I don't want to eat them," rerplied Heather.
"Get them down you, and you eat your carrots," she said turning to Nicky nastily. Nicky looked down at her carrots that glowed orange in her face. She then looked up at her mother implor-ingly.
"If you don't eat your carrots you won't be able to see in the dark," said Mrs Firk.
Each child sat at the table imprisoned by Mrs Firk's orders. They each stared down at their vegetables which refused to move until Mr Firk's mischievous fingers scooped up a load and wrapped it in a nap-kin and threw it in the bin. Feeling replenished, Mr Firk got up out of his chair and left for the pub.

A gust of wind swept across the town; drinkers were being shown the door by publicans up and down the high-street. The wind blew across the lawn and into the house through the open door. Mr Firk staggered through the doorway smelling of alcohol and tobacco. He trudged up the stairs careful not to make a noise in his intoxicated clumsiness. Mrs Firk sat knitting, aware but not acting. The clickity-click of her needles consciously silenced the creak-creak of the floor boards. He reached the top of the stairs; he turned one way and then another; he crept into Julie's room, pushed open the door and staggered around its edge.

He touched her blanket and crept underneath. She lay there transfixed by his calling. He rubbed himself up against her as she lay there dead to the world, neither asleep or awake:
"It's because I love you so much," he said.
She disappears inside herself. She envelopes herself in compliance because she does not want to hurt her dad; she does not want to hurt his feelings, but inside her other self she is saying, "go, go, go away, leave me alone."

It split. It divided. He went in through one door and in through another. Heather lay motion-less waiting for the devilish had of fate to tickle her to sleep. She waited; it went in and out of her; it approached another entrance but it had not entered the door at the very end of the cor-ridor.

Julie was fighting; she kicked him, scratched him and spat back at him. He turned to Heather; she had sympathy for her sister but she just wanted to get out. "Your special, more than Julie... you mustn't tell though. You wouldn't want daddy to go to prison now would you?"
She didn't feel comfortable with what her dad was doing but she didn't want him to get into trouble. So she took that trouble herself, inside her. She became two people; one that took the trouble and one that lived on top hiding the one below smothering her cries.

Nicky lay distracted. She could hear the wind rattling the doors and the windows and the bedstead, and she thought it could possibly, with a great heave ho thrust, bang through her door at any moment and with that lay bare a siege; a torrent of hell bound energy that would scoop her-up, terrorize her leaving her cold and naked and all alone.

She lay there untouched and innocent for the foreseeable. It would not be long, however, before she would join Heather at the big school. Mrs Standard would be there waiting for her, prepared, her mind ready to determine what a bad sort she was, for she could not alter what was predestined, she was a Firk. Mrs Standard had already set her level and Nicky was so well versed to one so much different. She was already excluded with little chance of success but who cares?

Mrs Firk sat down stairs knitting with greater fury. She switched on the telly and sat watching the shopping channel. Currency, money, that was something she could immerse herself in. She enjoyed losing herself in the world of ruthless exchange, where there is no emotion or sentiment. Everything is just fine because its business. And with that word every scurrilous deal, every underhand dealing is given an outward appearance of respectability.
She tried once; she knew it wasn't right but she wasn't particularly the maternal type. She had a memory that haunted her. Julie pulled on her night robe and complained that daddy had hurt her, down there in between her legs. She told her to be strong, not to cry and that she would tell daddy not to do it again.
"It's not right," she said.
He sat in his chair incandescent with rage. He gripped the chair that he sat in with intensity as he turned a bright shade of scarlet. He got up without acknowledging her presence or words. He went down to the pub and when he returned he struck her across the face and told her never to interfere with his love for

his daughters. Since that day she had told the girls that dad's visits were dreams that they must put to the back of their minds.

Above all else they must not breathe a word about what happens behind their door because if anyone found out, daddy would go to prison, mummy would not be able to cope and they would be put into care. If they were to go into care there would be nobody to look after them and they would have no future with no job and no chance of future happiness. Everything must be kept quiet and everything would work itself out in the end.

As the pubs closed the young and wanting to be young made their way to the city clubs. Rev-ellers drank copious amounts of larger, breezers and alco-pops intent upon losing their minds. Some to wipe out their misery, others to have fun, and others did not know why and others because that's what you do of a night time in the UK. Club owners rubbed their hands, clubbers emptied their pockets whilst countless thousands woke up to a world of poverty. The bang bang of the base resounded around the club vibrating through the floor and echoing around the world. Each little foot-step contributed to the over-all din which drove the world spinning on its axis. Spinning and losing control until bodies fell to the pavement and choked; jets of sickness pouring out over the pavement and into the gutter where shoppers would find themselves dodging in the morning.

Chapter 15: The Event, Mania and Delusions

Joseph woke early that morning. He did some work before school and set off with time to spare. It was a beautiful morning; the sky was blue, there wasn't a cloud to be seen and the birds were chirping. Sitting down at his desk in his classroom, the cleaners were pleasantly surprised to find Joseph in so early. His presence seemed to be recognition of the toil that the cleaners endured; toil that went unappreciated for the most part and ridiculed by the children remorselessly. He bore witness to their long hours, low pay and wrinkled faces.

Emma would be in school for perhaps the last time today. She was coming towards the end of her exam period. She was not going to continue her education at St Mary's School so Joseph had decided to tell her how he felt, how he felt about her to her face. She held a special place in his heart and he wanted to tell her before she left. She had said "hi," to him since the note but he wanted to push it further. He had read horoscope which had said to take risks and so he had taken that advice on board. The job had forced him to be assertive but he now lacked a ceiling.

Joseph had a number of errands to run before staff briefing to ensure his lessons for that day ran smoothly. He did some photocopying which took him to middle school, he then went to lower school to organise his form class reports as they were due out that day. Having carefully compiled each report for dispatch, from him to the pupils, and from them to the parents, Joseph strolled back to his teaching room in upper school.

It was down to chance that he happened to bump into Mr Goodlife, Head of Year Nine. It oc-curred to Joseph

that this would be an ideal opportunity to inquire about Heather's back-ground.
"Morning," said Joseph.
"Morning," said Mr Goodlife.
"Do you know Heather Firk?" said Joseph dim-wittedly.
"Yes, I know Heather," said Mr Goodlife ironically.
"What's her background like?" said Joseph."Normal," said Mr Goodlife, "mum and dad togeth-er, perfectly normal."
At this, Joseph dropped his suspicions until…"Her sister went off the rails even earlier than Heather."
"What's the father like?" Said Joseph perplexed.
"Never met him," said Mr Goodlife with an unquestioning abruptness.
It was at this point that Joseph laid his suspicions bare. If he was wrong he was wrong and he hoped nothing bad would come of it, but he could not pretend that he had no suspicions just in case he was right. His fears were relayed to the relevant person, Mrs Faith the school chaplain, who then presumably set the procedures for such a scenario into action. Joseph had told Mr Goodlife that he thought Heather was being sexually abused.

Joseph remained agitated. He had not expected to come clean about his fears concerning Heather. His feelings for Emma jumbled with his general concern for the well being of the pupils at the school and specifically, Heather. He knew Emma would be sitting the second part of the exam in the technology department down the short corridor along the concourse. He knew this could be his last opportunity to let Emma know how he felt face to face.

He popped in and out of the staffroom onto the concourse, in and out, in and out. He was gripped by the dilemma; he wanted her to know and yet he knew that he would be contraven-ing the rules governing the conduct of the teaching staff if he did. He knew that he was not supposed to have feelings for a pupil and he knew that he must not on any account allow a pupil to know that he had feelings that he wasn't allowed to have.

He stepped out of the staffroom and stood in the middle of the concourse; nervous about what was to become of him. His palms sweated as he rubbed his moist thumbs against his finger ends. He gnawed at his already clipped finger nails. A few pupils were seated on a bench that ran along the corridor towards the exam room. The stairs loomed opposite projecting its steps to higher places. It seemed that they too were waiting.

Joseph walked down the corridor towards the exam room purposefully but he felt exposed. The past and the present seemed to be about to meet but what of the future? The corridor was dark. There were no windows admitting sunlight. Photographs and displays adorned the walls. Past pupils and their work bore witness to his motive.

He reached the double doors which had small windows at head height for an adult to peer through. He looked through the glass and saw Emma perched on a stool waiting having completed the exam. She and the other candidates sat in silence as speaking out was forbidden.
Joseph stepped part way into the exam room and broke the silence. He stood with the door half open with his head pushed through.
"Can I speak to you?" He asked.
"What for?" She answered with angst in her voice.
"Two secs, out here," he said and his eyes motioned towards the corridor, down the corridor into the central

expanse of the concourse where each corridor met and the stairs led off to higher places.
"She nodded in agreement. Joseph turned around and departed through the door. It shut on him and he waited in the corridor.

The papers were collected. They were piled up in order of their candidate number which was clearly visible on the back of their seat. They would be judged by the examiner and a grade would be awarded. As they were dismissed permission was granted to them to speak. Emma headed off through the door and down the corridor unaware of Joseph's purpose. He was there waiting amongst some other pupils. Joseph braced himself:
"This hasn't happened to me before," he said, looking up at her for he was slouched down half on and half off the bench, "I love you."
"What?" she said with disdain and disbelief.
"I love you," he said again but with more purpose and with a look that she could not ignore.
She walked off unable to comprehend what she had just heard: a teacher proclaiming his love for her. She could not believe what she had just experienced for her interest in him was just a bit of fun confined only to the English classroom. She headed off across the concourse only to look half back saying, "Geek mate." She went past the stairs and down the corridor towards the main exit: for she was soon to leave compulsory education and start her own life. She burst out of the doors and into the brilliant sunshine. The sun was beating down, the sky was a radiant blue and not a cloud could be seen all around but it was too hot and brilliant for Joseph.

Joseph stood perplexed. She did not want him; she did not care about what he felt; she was caught totally unaware. He did not know what to do. What was there to do? Nothing, just carry on with what came before. He rubbed his head and pursed his lips. He looked this way and that totally confused. He collected himself. He had brought the Year Seven reports over to organise for he had yet to put each report for each pupil in their respective envelopes ready for dispatch.

He ascended the stairs and sat at his desk in his classroom with the reports before him. He was required to put each child's report in the envelope with their name on it and then he was to make two piles; one for the boys and one for the girls. His mind was all of a tizzy. He could not concentrate. The wrong report was going in the right envelope, the right report was going in the wrong envelope, the girls were mixed up with the boys and the boys mixed up with the girls. He could not separate, distinguish, compile and impose order on this unholy mess. His mind kept flitting backwards and forwards, in and out, how could he continue?

Mrs Standard stood at his door. She filled the space completely. She loomed large in Jo-seph's presence.
"Joseph, would you come with me please? The Head Teacher would like to see you in his office," said Mrs Standard.
"About Heather," said Joseph hopefully.
"No, it's not about Heather," said Mrs Standard who was not going to hear that tale.
Joseph stepped into Mr A Differ's office. It was larger than Mrs Standard's but more formal. Mr A Differ sat rather stiffly behind his desk with a stern look on his face. Joseph sat opposite the Head Teacher and Mrs Standard, his Deputy sat beside him. Mr A Differ sat in judgement whilst Mrs Standard spoke.
"We've had a complaint Joseph. We've just received a phone call from Mrs Bylaw who is very upset. She says that you have made an advance towards her

daughter Emma. She says that you waited for her to finish her exam and then you told her that you love her. Is this true?"

Joseph stuttered. He knew it was true but he did not want to tell them so.

"Noooow, yes it's true, I did it," said Joseph embarrassed.

"Well, Joseph," said Mrs Standard with an ingratiating smile, "how long have you felt like this?"

"Oooh, I don't know. A while," said Joseph whilst Mr A Differ sat watching.

"And what did you hope to achieve by telling Emma of your feelings?" said Mrs Standard who was suddenly reminded of the time when she first started dating.

"I didn't want her to go, not without her knowing," said Joseph.

"You didn't want her to go," she said, "arhh," she purred, "so you wanted to see her?"

Joseph smiled and shrugged and in that smile he seemed to say, "yes." His shrug ceiled his fate. He looked up at Mrs Standard, like a child to a mother, for he needed help. Mrs Stand-ard sat with a straight back and projecting bust. She peered down at him and said, "you fell in love with her and you wanted her, they're human emotions, it happens, things happen in schools which we cannot legislate for, and with that she looked up at the cross on the wall which fell out of focus as she turned to the window.

Joseph did not contradict her. Mr A Differ had a decision to make. He bowed to the inevitable. He could not have a teacher proclaiming his love for a pupil. He knew there would be talk. Joseph had declared his love openly, there was not the slightest possible chance that this could be kept quiet, and there was Mrs Bylaw to contend with. It would set the school community alive with gossip and intrigue.

"This is very serious matter, Joseph I cannot pretend that this has not happened. Now I think it will be best for all if you pack your things and go home. We'll have to investigate this matter thoroughly and come to a conclusion based on the evidence."

And with that Joseph was gone. The doors shut decisively behind him and he was gone. The sky was a brilliant blue and the sun was beating down upon him.

Chapter 16: Rules

Mr A Differ was at a loss about what to do. He had been in the teaching profession for over thirty years but nothing quite like this had happened before. He had no rules for such an event, no procedure by which to follow. He knew that there were procedures in place but what with this being so unusual (the declaration about Heather and then Emma within a few hours) and he being a new Head Teacher he was not familiar with the set protocol. He put down his pen and left for the Education Division at the County Hall to seek advice.

The facts had yet to be established but Joseph had admitted to making an advance towards a pupil that was nothing to do with the job. He had to act; he had to treat this event with the up most seriousness. He did not know what was going on in Joseph's mind; he did not know him from Adam; it could not be ignored.

Firstly an internal and external educational authority investigation needed to be enacted. Secondly the social services needed to be informed and thirdly the police had to be notified. Mr A Differ had to get back now that he knew the rules to follow. He was due to see Mrs Bylaw, the witnesses and the other representatives of the authorities. Emma had told her mother that she did not wish to return to the school and so she remained safe and uninvolved at home.

Mrs Bylaw was furious; she was incandescent with rage. No adult was going to upset her daughter and escape punishment least of all a teacher who was supposed to be helping her with her education. She pulled up into a space in her crime busting mobile and slammed the door; she marched over to the school main entrance at furious pace having activated the cen-tral locking; she grabbed the door handle and flung

it open and in she went, past Heather Firk who was invisible to her, and over to reception.
"Mrs Bylaw, I'm here to see the Head Teacher," she said with furious indignation.
"Arhh yes, Mr Differ is waiting for you, if you would like to go straight into his office.
She marched past the brown chairs; the door was open ready for her arrival." Mr Differ invited her to sit down where Joseph had sat only just before. He shut the door and braced himself; he knew that if he did not handle this carefully the shit was going to hit the fan big style and we can't have shit in the Head-Master's office now can we? Shit all over the strawberry coloured wall paper, shit splattered all over the framed photographs that adorned the walls, shit on the desk, trodden into the carpet, no, it would not do.

Mrs Bylaw's head was bright red and if anything tended towards a deep purple colour. "What on earth is going on at this school? How can you allow a man of such motives go near my daughter? This man should not be allowed near children for goodness sake""
"Yes, we realise that this is a very grave matter and we are treating it with the utmost serious-ness."
"My daughter is trying to do her GCSEs and this man who is supposed to be her teacher has other things on his mind. She's a child for goodness sake and he's, he's thinking of goodness knows what. It's disgusting! I won't stand for it. I want him removed from this school. He's not to teach for another day! Emma's afraid to come in do you know!"
"We realise the situation is very serious."
"I don't know if you do!" she stormed, "You don't seem to know what your staff are up to."
"We…"
"I have to take the afternoon off work and bring this to your attention. My daughter is sat at home frightened

to come into school! And this, this when she should be concentrating fully on her GCSE exams. How is she supposed to focus on her studies when a member of your staff is coming on to her?" she boomed going a deeper purple if at all possible.

"We do not question the impropriety that has occurred but we…"

"Impropriety, I'll give you impropriety. He ought to be hung, drawn and quartered for what he has done. I'm not having my daughter being sexually harassed. This is an outrage, an abso-lute outrage."

"I understand your anger and agree that measures need to be taken but we.."

"But? They're no buts about it. This man is not fit to teach. I'm not having that man in this school whilst my daughter is a pupil here! Do you understand me?"

"I understand you perfectly well. I am well aware that measures need to be taken but we need to establish the facts in order to justify any actions that need to be taken."

"She's only just turned sixteen. She's a child."

"This is what we have done. We've arranged to see you, we arranged to see the witnesses to the incident and we have notified social services and the police so that we can get to the bot-tom of this. Do not be under any illusions that we are in any way treating this situation lightly."

"I trust you can assure me that he will not be setting foot on the premises?"

"We need to establish the facts…"

"The facts, the facts is my daughter has been subject to a sexual advance by one of your members of staff! What more do you need to know?"

"We can't.."

"You bloody well can. My daughter has exams to sit! She is not coming to school knowing that he, he might at any time, at any moment creep up behind her. There is no telling what he might do."

"Of course, Emma's education is of primary importance to us."
"So I trust he will not be here."
"We will make arrangements to ensure that he will not be here and he will not disrupt Emma's final days at this school, but in order to deal with this situation properly we will need to estab-lish the facts."
"He won't be here?"
"No."
"Thank you. Why it has taken this long I do not know."
"You can rest assured that the member of staff concerned will not be in school. I now need to speak to the relevant authorities and take steps on their advice."
"I want to be kept informed about each development."
"I will let you know the outcome of the interviews. May I offer my sincerest apology and regret for this alarming situation. Every effort will be made to ensure that Emma can ease back into the last week of her time here."
"Just make sure that he is not here so it can't affect her."
"I think, for Emma's benefit, we need to keep this under wraps. If we are not careful we will distress and cause her more trauma by creating a scene. By the fact that she has chosen not to come in suggests she is upset by the repercussions."
"She must come first."
"Precisely, and that's why we need to keep her focussed on her exams rather than involving her with more worries concerning how far reaching this incident is going to be. What I suggest is that I shall suspend the member of staff concerned indefinitely, so that Emma can complete her studies, we can complete our investigation and then we can take appropriate action according to the law and rules governing conduct."

"Make sure of it," and with that Mrs Bylaw left the school. She was exhausted. She pulled away in her crime-busting mobile.

Chapter 17: Exclusion

Everybody except for Joseph was enjoying a prolonged spell of warm sunny days. The field basked in sunshine and kids enjoyed the freedom it provided. Having broken the rules, Jo-seph was told to go home. He was not to return to school as he could not be trusted to oper-ate within the remit governing the educational institution concerning staff conduct. Joseph was formally suspended from duty and the school made it clear that he would not be welcome on the premises again. The police and social services were no longer involved because Joseph had not attempted to touch Emma but he was due to attend a disciplinary hearing at County Hall designed to investigate the matter and pass judgement. He sat inside of his flat alone. The curtains were drawn and he awaited his fate in darkness.

Joseph had a few days to prepare for the meeting at which he would be given the opportunity to relate his side of events. He was however somewhat in the dark over the exact nature of proceedings: who would be there, what the exact charge he was facing and how the charges would be put. He knew that he had joked with the children in a way that might be considered unprofessional and he knew that his declaration of love constituted his crimes and so he de-cided to make a statement detailing each separate incident and the circumstances under which they occurred.

Mr A Differ had to be seen to be in a position of impartiality in order to preside over proceed-ings. He therefore had had no contact with Joseph since his suspension. Mrs Standard pro-vided the source of contact. She had contacted Joseph to inform him of his suspension, the disciplinary hearing to follow and she had drawn Joseph into talking his way into trouble.

She had suggested to Joseph that he might be better off if he had his family for support but it had never once occurred to her that he had never had a particularly close relationship with them built on trust and understanding. And on that morning of his judgement, she sat down at her desk in her rather cosy office and picked up the telephone:
"Hello," said Joseph.
"Morning," said Mrs Standard, "have I just woken you up?" she asked.
"No," said Joseph," having been up all night.
"I'm just ringing to wish you good luck and to say that we're all praying for you."
"Thank you," said Joseph.
"I also would like to ask you because Mrs Grouch has asked me to ask you, whether you can bring any outstanding work belonging to the school or the pupils, into the hearing today."
"Yes," said Joseph, "but I haven't marked it all yet."
"Don't worry about that if you could just bring it in."
And with that settled the point of contact ended. Joseph washed himself clean and dressed himself smartly. He picked up his statement, locked the door of his empty flat and set out to County Hall.

Joseph had a vague idea where County Hall stood. There was a concentration of municipal buildings in the centre of town. He drove into town to a centrally located car park. As he pulled up to the entrance he found that the barrier that usually lay horizontal denying access and demanding charge, was vertical inviting admittance. He drove on through and manoeuvred his car into a space.

He locked the car and walked off in the direction of the municipal buildings. When he reached the first intimidating building, he stepped inside and asked at reception whether this was, or where he might find County Hall division D.

"No, this isn't D, you need to turn around go out of the door and down to your left and it's the first intimidating building on your right, okay?" she told him.

"Yes, thank you very much, most helpful," replied Joseph.

He followed her instructions and stepped inside the second intimidating building. He went up to reception and asked if this was County Hall division D.

"No, this is division C," she said.

"arhh," said Joseph, "could you tell me where I might find D?

"Yes, you go back out of the door, and continue around to the left."

"Thank you," said Joseph.

He did an about turn and marched off out towards the left. When he reached the third intimi-dating building all panic had been let loose. Bells were ringing continuously. A loud piercing noise rang out from the centre of town penetrating the mid-day sky. It was coming from the heart of the building and it sent its occupants scurrying; fleeing the scene to avoid the fire.

Indeed, they were evacuating the building. One by one they emptied out into the street; through the big doors, men, women, black, white, able, disabled, rich, poor clever and stupid, out onto the pavement across the road and onto the grassy clearing. They each lined-up in their places ready to be accounted for. Joseph looked up at the grey imposing building. Bells rang out loudly in his ears. A security guard stood by the doors. Joseph approached him:

"Is this County Hall division D? he asked.

The security guard looked over his head and did not move.

"Is this County Hall division D?" he asked competing with the cacophony emanating from in-side.

"I can't hear you," replied the security guard.
"Is this County Hall, Division D," Joseph thundered and at that moment the heavens opened.

Great cracks split the sky, an almighty rumble tore across the town, rain lashed down where-upon umbrellas popped up. Some people got wet, others were protected, and then from the corner of his eye he sore Mr A. Differ accompanied by a lady he did not recognise. They en-tered the building through a brownish black back door. He knew he was in the right place.

As if in some kind of collusion the rain and the alarm ceased at the same moment. The public servants who hid under their umbrellas became aware that the onslaught had passed and slowly but surely the umbrellas came down. They grew in confidence, exchanged pleasantries and strolled back into the building two by two.

Joseph had to wait for the employees to get into position before he could gain admittance. Nobody must enter until they were ready with their rules, regulations, protocol, and method. They had to shuffle their papers, fill out their forms and twitch with their pens at the ready. Names, details and signatures it all had to be recorded.

Joseph approached the reception area. He had to put his name down and the lady behind the desk issued him with a visitors pass. He was then directed to a room down a corridor and round a bend. He found Mr A Differ sat behind a table and the lady who was from the Local Educational Authority sat adjacent. They stood with purpose as if the proceedings had already been decided as Joseph entered and then they sat

together. Mr A Differ manoeuvred his buttocks, leaned forward and initiated proceedings.
"The purpose of the meeting is to investigate allegations of gross misconduct following inappropriate behaviour towards a female pupil. Could you please explain your actions surround-ing this incident."
"Yes, I have prepared a statement detailing each incident for your consideration."
And so Joseph began the tiresome business of raking over each time he had compromised his professionalism. He left nothing out and he left himself open to their mercy. Finding the whole episode an ordeal, Mr A Differ, noting his obvious distress intervened:
"Would you like to pause? Get a breath of fresh air?"
"Yes, if that's okay."
"Would you like to excuse yourself and meet back here in five minutes?"
"Thank you."
Joseph appreciated the offer. He stood-up, turned around and walked through the corridors wiping his eyes and out through the door out onto the street. The air was fresh although it was still damp from the storm. The grass was greener but the birds were rather annoyed that they had gotten wet. Joseph walked over to the nearby newsagent and bought a small bottle of water and a packet of tissues. He took a refreshing gulp and dried his eyes.

He turned around and headed back to the intimidating building. Again he dabbed his eyes and it was as he brought the tissue down and he looked up that his eyes picked out Lucy Klass from his Year Eleven class, walking along the opposite pavement. She was looking at him but although he saw her it did not register at first. He bowed down and something dropped into place. He looked up at her and realised who it was. She looked sadly at him: "hi sir," she said imploringly, Joseph smiled and waved at her. She seemed to say it was alright and that he was not to blame. He somehow felt exonerated.

Joseph, faced by the security guard, stepped in through the doors, down the corridor and into the room from which he had come. He sat down in the seat vacated only minutes before; he picked up his statement, confessed it all and offered his resignation. Mr A Differ waited until Joseph had finished. He shifted his buttocks, lent forward and reluctantly accepted his resig-nation or so he said. The lady then asked Joseph to sign and date the statement and give it the status of a letter of resignation. Joseph duly obliged and his time at St Mary's was officially over.

Chapter 19: Justice? An Ending?

The day was strangely silent. The birds had taken a break from their mating calls; the cars were running smoothly and the bad tempered felt languid for once and forgot to slam their horns at the sign of human weakness or culpability. In school, there were signs situated out-side the halls demanding silence as exams were in progress and curtains were drawn across windows to prevent the sun dazzling pupil effort and concentration.

Past the hall on the left and the technology room on the right, through the concourse and into the senior management corridor, Heather stepped nervously into a room. She sat down at ta-ble where two female social workers sat opposite:
"Would you like to take a seat Heather? This won't take long. It's nothing to worry about. We've just got a few questions to ask you. Is that okay?
"Okay," said Heather mistrustfully.
"We notice that you often find it difficult to keep out of trouble in school. Can you tell us why that is?"
"I just don't like some of the rules."
"And what is it about the rules you dislike?"
"There stupid."
"What do you find stupid about them?"
"I don't know there just stupid."
"Can you give me an example of a rule you dislike?"
"Why should I have to wear school uniform because you say? It's not like I'm hurting anyone if I don't."
"Why would you want to be different?"
"I don't know. Why do you want to know?"
"Do you prefer it at home? Where you don't have to wear uniform?"
"I just like to be myself."
"How is your home life?"

"It's fine. I don't know why you're asking these questions."
"We're almost done now. When children have problems at home there are ways to solve those problems. Is there anything at home you don't like?"
"Like what?"
"So there is nothing?"
"You do feel able to tell us if there was don't you?"
"Yes."
"Okay, we don't need to keep you any longer. Thanks for your time. Off you go."
Heather left the room in the senior management area of upper school quite confused. She stepped into the concourse and passed the stairs to higher places wondering where all the interest had come from.

When Heather got home she confided in Julie. Julie hated what her father had done to her; how he had taken away her childhood before it had really started. The thought of him going to prison did not disturb her; it filled her with pleasure. She could not however bring herself to talk about what he had done; she kept it hidden inside her. Heather was alarmed when her sister just shrugged her shoulders and left the room. Julie sat on the couch and watched the television not caring whether her father had been rumbled or not. After all, the damage for her had already been done.

Heather felt something had to be done and so she turned to her mother:
"Mum, at school today I had to answer questions to some people I didn't know," confessed Heather.
"What do you mean questions," replied Mrs Firk.
"Questions.." returned Heather.
"What are you talking about Heather," said Mrs Firk with more force and interest.
"Two ladies wanted to know whether everything was okay," said Heather elaborating further.

"And what did you say," said Mrs Firk with a stern look on her face.

"I didn't tell them anything," said Heather.

"You said everything is fine because it is fine?" said Mrs Firk looking to be corroborated.

"Yes," said the outer Heather nodding.

"Has anything unusual happened at school that might had led to this, Heather. I want you to think very hard about this. Has anyone in school been asking you questions or behaving unusually in anyway? Any of the teachers?" said Mrs Firk becoming more alarmed as she thought.

"Hmmmmm…"

"Anything. Think hard. This is important."

"Well my Study Skills teacher is a bit different from the rest. He talks to us more normally and he likes to give work that we like to do. He lets us speak our minds."

"You haven't spoken your mind have you?" said Mrs Firk suddenly horrified.

"No," said Heather suddenly realising the implications of what she had admitted

"Okay, calm down. Everything's fine. It is fine, that's what you told them isn't it?"

"Yes"

"Tell me, what do you know about your Study Skills teacher? What's his name first?"

And so Heather sat down with her mum and told her all about Joseph. All the conversations they had had, how he treated the class as a whole and how he conducted himself at school.

Mrs Firk resolved to wait till the morning before informing her husband for he might be drunk. She could not risk telling him when he returned from the pub; there would be no telling what he might do with a full tank on board. She needed to tell him in order to ensure that he did not do anything to arouse further suspicion. She would not be able to bear the indignity of a scandal surrounding her family.

She waited for the right moment and gently made him aware of the situation careful not to incur his wrath:

"A teacher's been sniffing round asking Heather questions," said Mrs Firk.

"What questions," said Mr Firk sternly.

"Questions. About home," said Mrs Firk trying to make him see the possible seriousness of events.

"Everything's fine," said Mr Firk suddenly shouting, "what's she said?"

"She said everything's fine, as you said."

"Good, everything is fine," said Mr Firk relaxing."

"Who is this teacher?" said Mr Firk angry that anyone could have the audacity to poke their nose into his family affairs. "Is he local?"

"He lives in hope village."

"So he could be looking out for us, couldn't he? Which street?"

"I don't know."

"Well what do you know? Dammit woman this could be important!"

"He lives in a top floor flat and he drives an older white escort."

"And what's he look like?"

"Short hair, late twenties, slim, a bit below average height. He's got a stranger's accent."

"Well if he comes snooping round here I'll be ready for him. Fucking up-start."

"Maybe you should pay him a little visit," suggested Mrs Firk.

"What do you mean a little visit," said Mr Firk accusingly.

"You know, warn him off. Show him you've got balls and he can't fuck around with us."

And with that Mr Firk left the breakfast table comforted that he knew all he needed to know. Heather wouldn't want him to go to prison and he sure as hell wasn't going to let anyone come between him and his liberty.

Mr Firk had started drinking early that day. He stopped off at a bar as soon as it had opened. He worked himself up into a rage and got into his car, shut the door and pulled on his seat belt. Sufficiently restrained, he pushed the gear stick forward and set off for hope village. When he got there he drove up and down each street in search of an older type white escort. After scoring a few misses, he pulled into a residential car park and there it was. He turned around again and drove up and down all the other streets comprising Hope village. There was no other car of this sort, so carefully ensuring that he was not being watched, he cruised back to the car park.

He pulled up alongside the white escort and walked around it and then he marched up to the communal door. He figured number one must be at the bottom therefore he must live at num-ber five or six. He pressed the buzzer for number six. There was no answer. He tried number five.
"Hello," said Joseph.
"Hello, water-board, I've come to check a reported leek. Can you open the door?"
"Yes."
And with that Joseph pressed the buzzer and Mr Firk stepped in. Joseph assumed that the leek must be in the communal area and thinking that he could be of no more assistance, he stepped into his hallway. He suddenly felt an over-whelming need to have a dump so he en-tered his bathroom. He opened the door and dropped his trousers and pants and sat down on his toilet. He heaved and pain reeked through his body. Shit started pummelling through his arse cheeks when he heard fate knock at the door.

"I can't come to the door right now," said Joseph in anguish.

Mr Firk was in no mood to be denied. He had come this far, he was not about to turn round and walk out of the block with this unresolved. He put his right hand up against the door whilst his left hand pushed down on the handle and in he went; a gust of wind following him down the hall way. The toilet door stood open. Joseph sat exhausted. Mr Firk turned as he approached the toilet. He glanced in expecting it to be empty. Joseph looked up in disbelief as Mr Firk stood before him. Overcome by a feeling of revulsion, Mr Firk bent over and grabbed Joseph by the throat. Joseph struggled but he was too weak. He turned and his dirty bottom lent into Mr Firk's crotch. Joseph's head went a purple colour as Mr Firk tightened the fatal grip around his neck. Joseph's head went limp. Blood oozed out of his mouth and nose. Mr Firk gently placed him back on the toilet and kissed him lovingly. He then turned around and left wiping away the prints left on the door handle.

A few hours later Mrs Bylaw stepped in through the half open door. She pushed the door to and smudged the only finger-print left by Mr Firk. She found the body and walked around it unsympathetically:

"There's a body in here. You best call the station. He's been strangled whilst having a shit. How rude, surely he could have waited till he'd finished."

The light faded; the evening sky descended. The darkness came and past, dawn approached and the postman set about his work, dropping off different messages through the myriad doors, what they contained, he did not know. Parents woke their children and sent them packing off to school, Joseph lay in a coffin-like filing cabinet in the hospital morgue.

News of Joseph's death was quick to spread across the school. Teachers and pupils found it difficult to digest the information but it gave them all so much to talk about. Mrs Faith had God on her side so she was best placed to offer words of comfort and tranquillity: "In our time of need, Dear Lord, let us remember and celebrate the happier times of our dear and departed former colleague," she dipped and rose, "let us pray for a brighter future, a brighter world than the one that Joseph tragically came face to face with, Lord in your mercy, Hear our prayer.

The End

www.ingramcontent.com/pod-product-compliance
Ingram Content Group UK Ltd.
Pitfield, Milton Keynes, MK11 3LW, UK
UKHW041945230426
12048UKWH00008B/138